Grade 2

Writing in the Content Areas

Prewriting · Drafting · Revision · Editing

Social Studies · Health · Science · Math · Art

Editor
Kim Fields

Illustrator
Vicky Frazier

Cover Artist
Tony Carrillo

Managing Editor
Ina Massler Levin, M.A.

Creative Director
Karen J. Goldfluss, M.S. Ed.

Art Production Manager
Kevin Barnes

Art Coordinator
Renée Christine Yates

Imaging
Craig Gunnell
James Edward Grace

Publisher
Mary D. Smith, M.S. Ed.

Authors

Garth Sundem, M. M.
Kristi Pikiewicz

Teacher Created Resources, Inc.
6421 Industry Way
Westminster, CA 92683
www.teachercreated.com

ISBN-13: 978-1-4206-9042-2
ISBN-10: 1-4206-9042-6

© 2006 Teacher Created Resources, Inc.
Made in U.S.A.

Teacher Created Resources

Table of Contents

Table of Contents *(cont.)*

Why Content-Area Writing?

We live in the Age of Information according to many experts. Global travel, satellites, computers and the Internet, and advanced technologies are changing the way we live and communicate.

And we owe it to our students to prepare them the best we can to interact with the world of today, as well as tomorrow. Students must be able to clearly express their thoughts and ideas in writing, not just to do well in language arts, but to demonstrate their understanding in other subjects as well. That means written communication in all the content areas—math, science, and social studies—is just as important as poetry and fiction.

Most likely, you have already given writing assignments to your students in math, science, and social studies classes: lab reports, posters, word problems, diagrams, journals, graphs, or research projects. These are all examples of content-area writing.

However, by looking at your content-area assignments as writing assignments and applying to these assignments the same teaching techniques you use in your writing class, you can teach the skills of expression necessary to the real-world use of your content area and reinforce your content area materials in the process.

Your integrated curriculum will help the students learn the skills of the integrated world.

Down the road, the students will recall your math assignment in which they made posters and explained graphing techniques when preparing marketing plans. Your health class opinion paper will help the students when, years down the line, they want to write a letter to the editor of their local paper about the effects of secondhand smoke. Especially in the Digital Age, the students need to learn to express themselves through writing. Whether it is medicine, business, entrepreneurship, or middle management, smart writing will help the students succeed.

That being said, it is not your job to mold the next Dr. Seuss. However, it is certainly appropriate to ask the students to write about the effects of air pollution on the environment—and the style of this writing should be appropriate to your assignment. It should be functional, clear, informative, and be presented in a manner that communicates ideas effectively. By teaching writing in the content areas, you can help the students work toward this goal.

In this book we will consider the term *writing* to mean "expression on the page." Writing takes a wide variety of forms: annotated diagrams, cartoon strips, charts, lists, notes, and many more. In a nutshell, writing in the content areas should enhance not only writing abilities, but should first and foremost help the students comprehend, retain, and interact with your subject area materials.

No matter what the content area (math, social studies, art, health, or science), writing will bridge the gap between your teaching and demonstration of student understanding. You may assess students' writing in two ways: with an emphasis on an understanding of the subject matter and the way in which the students communicate this understanding.

How to Use This Book

In the Theory and Assessment sections of this book, techniques are offered for teaching writing in the content areas. They include the following:

- the Writing Process in the content areas
- content area writing assessment: using the Traits of Good Writing with emergent writers

If these terms are familiar to you, you will be able to use the techniques after reviewing the relevant chapters as a refresher.

If the Traits of Good Writing or the Writing Process is completely new to you, you may want to supplement this book with further study using one of the many published in-depth references.

The second half of this book is made up of units and lesson plans, ranging from tips on designing your own content area writing projects to ready-to-use assignments. Ideally, you would ask the students to complete the assignments using the Writing Process and evaluate them using the Traits of Good Writing. However, you may use the lessons with whatever writing strategies are most comfortable. Lessons are nonsequential—you can pick and choose from them as you like.

Again, the techniques and lessons presented in this book are meant to help you reinforce your content area material while asking the students to express their command of this material in effective writing.

Each lesson requires one to three class periods to complete. As all lessons include a writing component, the National Writing Standards met by each lesson are referenced on pages 6–7. Additional content area standards are listed individually.

The final section of this book includes graphic organizers that you may use for any occasion. These diagrams, brainstorming sheets, organizers, and more can help the students as they proceed through the steps of the Writing Process.

Standards for Writing (Grades K–2)

Most states have published standards to guide teachers as to what is expected of students at various grade levels. The following is a generic list of writing standards. To find the specific standards for your school district, contact your state's department of education. Usually, these standards are available on the Internet or from your district education office. This page and page 7 reference the universal collection of standards synthesized by John S. Kendall and Robert J. Marzano in their book *Content Knowledge: A Compendium of Standards and Benchmarks for K–12 Education* (Second Edition, 1997). This book is published jointly by McRel (Mid-continent Regional Educational Laboratory, Inc.) and ASCD (Association for Supervison and Curriculum Development). (Used by permission of McRel.) Specific descriptions of each standard follows.

1. Uses the general skills and strategies of the Writing Process
   A. Prewriting: Uses prewriting strategies to plan written work
   B. Drafting and Revising: Uses strategies to draft and revise written work
   C. Editing and Publishing: Uses strategies to edit and publish written work
   D. Evaluates own and others' writing
   E. Uses strategies to organize written work
   F. Uses writing and other methods to describe familiar persons, places, objects, or experiences
   G. Writes in a variety of forms or genres

2. Uses the stylistic and rhetorical aspects of writing
   A. Uses descriptive words to convey basic ideas

3. Uses grammatical and mechanical conventions in written compositions
   A. Uses conventions of print in writing
   B. Uses complete sentences in written compositions
   C. Uses nouns in written compositions
   D. Uses verbs in written compositions
   E. Uses adjectives in written compositions
   F. Uses adverbs in written compositions
   G. Uses conventions of spelling in written compositions
   H. Uses conventions of capitalization in written compositions
   I. Uses conventions of punctuation in written compositions

Standards For Writing (Grades K-2) *(cont.)*

4. Gathers and uses information for research purposes
   A. Generates questions about topics of personal interest
   B. Uses a variety of sources to gather information
5. Uses listening and speaking strategies for different purposes
   A. Makes contributions in class and group discussions
   B. Asks and responds to questions
   C. Follows rules of conversation and group discussion
   D. Uses different voice level, phrasing, and intonation for different situations
   E. Uses level-appropriate vocabulary in speech
   F. Gives and responds to oral directions
   G. Recites and responds to familiar stories, poems, and rhymes with patterns
   H. Knows differences between language used at home and language used in school

Techniques of Content-Area Writing Instruction

This section discusses techniques for teaching writing in your content areas including the following:

- an introduction to content area writing

- the Writing Process in the content areas

- writing-based learning centers in the content areas

- content area writing assessment: using the Traits of Good Writing with emergent writers

- a model for introducing writing in your content area classes

What Is a "Writing-Based Content-Area Assignment"?

When you think of a writing assignment for science class, you might picture a detailed outline and many research note cards or a detailed diagram on a large sheet of poster board, complete with arrows, boxes, and labels. It might be that neither fits your plan for the upcoming student science project.

The point is, if your students put anything on paper, you have the basis for a writing-based content area assignment. In fact, with younger classes, "writing" in the content areas may not be writing at all—think of it more as "displaying information on a page," which will frequently include as much illustration as text. This definition of *writing*, like the visual projects you likely do in your language arts classes, will help prepare the students for more rigorous content area writing as their skills progress in later years. Thus, in this book, we will look at how to evaluate illustrations and emergent text as writing.

Examples of Writing-Based Content-Area Assignments

Math

- creating, illustrating, and presenting story problems ("If I had thirteen peaches and I took away five, ...")
- reading and creating basic bar graphs
- keeping a "What I Did Today in Math Class" journal to share with parents
- drawing geometric shapes found in the real world
- making hands-on math projects, such as dice-based board games (addition or subtraction), or group skits that demonstrate visual math ("The five of us were standing here and then Jenna and Joanne showed up. Now there are . . . .")

Science

- illustrating observations of the natural world
- keeping journals/notebooks (these may be illustrated)
- designing posters
- creating hypotheses ("I think that . . . .")
- listing experiment directions
- interacting with age-appropriate science magazines
- responding to short-answer questions

What Is a "Writing-Based Content-Area Assignment"? *(cont.)*

Examples of Writing-Based Content-Area Assignments *(cont.)*

Social Studies

- drawing during historical fiction that is read aloud (or illustrated responses to a picture book)
- working in groups to create a presentation about a multicultural holiday
- creating posters, notes, etc.
- drawing and labeling maps
- illustrating and titling scenes of historical events

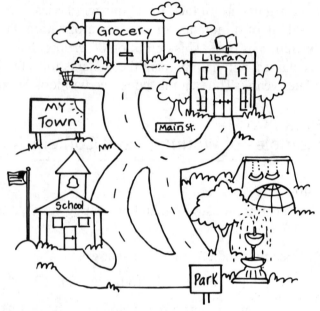

Health

- making anti-smoking posters
- drawing and labeling the rules for a made-up game
- listing the effects of certain good and bad health behaviors
- creating and illustrating healthful recipes
- making an illustrated list of healthful foods
- reflecting on team-building activities with titled drawings and discussion
- labeling three muscle sets in the human body
- drawing a picture of and titling a recent sports event in which they participated

Art

- selecting three feelings from a word bank that describe a painting
- writing a list of color words
- drawing portraits of famous artists, including a one-sentence caption
- creating and keeping an art journal with short descriptions of daily projects
- preplanning an art project (drawing or writing)
- including titles or written descriptions on art projects

The Goals of Content-Area Writing

Though integrating writing into your content area classes will certainly help the students improve their writing skills, the primary goal of these classes remains to teach content. In the time slot devoted to writing, you can teach the students skills they will then use in your content area classes.

Writing in the content areas should reinforce learning, rather than be an additional constraint on your time. Thus the goals of writing in the content areas are as follows:

- to reinforce content-area material

- to offer different modes of learning information

- to help the students learn to communicate ideas clearly

Writing to Reinforce Understanding

Putting thoughts on paper allows each student in your class to respond to your content area lessons. Perhaps you already do this in the format of an independent assignment that checks for understanding of a key concept you taught (e.g., assigning a math worksheet that asks students to apply a skill they learned in a lesson). In this example, you could also ask the students to keep a math journal and after each lesson, write and illustrate one thing they learned. This would be a content area writing assignment and would reinforce students' understanding of the material.

Writing can also take the form of notes. By using their own words in regard to content area information, the students will take an important step toward making it their own. With younger classes, you can even encourage notes to be illustrated (e.g., making a drawing of the planets, the differences between an insect and an arachnid, or the parts of the digestive system).

Writing to Demonstrate Understanding

You can also use writing to assess. This can be as general as asking the students to write three things they learned in the course of a lesson or as specific as having the students write responses to short-answer questions. With less experienced classes, you might have the students draw something you recently studied and label three parts of the illustration.

Finding Time for Content-Area Writing

As a teacher, the last thing you need is more to do. Consider replacing or revising some of your current practices, rather than trying to add content area writing on top of what you already do. With a little planning, you can find ways to insert writing without needing an extra 15 minutes for each class. For example, rather than starting class on Monday by asking the students what they did over the weekend, use this time for the students to quietly write or draw these events in journals. Or instead of having the students draw arrows from the parts of an insect to the correct term on a worksheet, have the students draw the insect and label the parts themselves. Instead of having the students complete a multiple-choice test, have them write short paragraphs, asking them to include the specific information you are assessing.

In both instruction and assessment, you can find ways to insert content area writing in place of (not in addition to) more traditional activities.

Narrative vs. Expository Text

The majority of the writing in your content area classes will be nonfiction expository writing. Instead of creating stories, the students will be using writing to convey meaning. This is not to say there is no place for a story about how food passes through the digestive system; but most of the time, you will ask the students to write expository text in your content area classes. In fact, with younger classes, one of your first challenges will be to explain the difference between fiction and nonfiction and demonstrate exactly what expository writing is. Let them know that expository writing tells information without giving an opinion. This gets tricky when expository writing includes a story line (e.g., an article for the class newspaper reporting on last Saturday's soccer game). Help the students see that expository writing is based on facts. In the example above, the article would be expository if it described exactly what happened during the soccer game, but would be narrative if, at the end of the game, aliens landed in midfield.

The following are examples of expository writing:

- newspaper article
- rules of a game
- book report
- description of things that actually happened
- how-to guide
- map
- letter
- journal entry
- notes
- interview
- definition

Teaching Students to Evaluate Content-Area Writing

This is where reading and writing overlap. Through evaluating their own writing, other students' work, and published examples, the students will gain a better idea of what works and what doesn't work in content area writing. However, you will need to equip the students with the tools to form an honest critique—at first they may not know what to look for or what vocabulary to use in describing how "good" or "bad" a piece of writing is. With a sample reading, you may offer the students specific criteria for use in evaluating its success, such as "Does the article contain who, what, where, when, and why?" or "After reading these two pages in the textbook, do you think you learned nothing, a little, some, a lot, or tons about Abraham Lincoln? Is there anything you wish the book had explained in more depth?" With other readings, you might ask the students to write short critiques using the vocabulary of the Traits of Good Writing (see pages 18–19).

Of course, evaluating content area writing utilizes the tools of content area reading. The students will need to know how to extract information from written text.

The following are a few ways to encourage the students to interact with written material.

Peer Group Sharing

Have the students form small groups in which authors share their work and others critique it. In this scenario, ask those critiquing to offer at least two positive comments for every piece of constructive criticism.

Summarizing an Article

In addition to helping the students solidify the article's content through putting it in their own words, they can present the information to the class and describe what they liked and did not like about the article.

Self-Critique

After finishing a writing project, have the students score themselves using the Traits of Good Writing.

A Quick Note on Reading in the Content Areas

As seen above, it is difficult to discuss writing without also including reading. While this book focuses specifically on writing, the following published resources will help you increase students' ability to read content area material:

- *Content Area Reading: Literacy and Learning Across the Curriculum* by Richard and Jo Anne Vacca (Allyn & Bacon, 2004)
- *Teaching Reading in Social Studies, Science, and Math* by Laura Robb (Teaching Resources, 2003)
- *Tools for Teaching Content Literacy* by Janet Allen (Stenhouse Publishers, 2004)
- *Subjects Matter: Every Teacher's Guide to Content-Area Reading* by Harvey Daniels and Steven Zemelman (Heinemann, 2004)

The Writing Process

All authors use the Writing Process to some degree in every piece they write, though not always in a linear fashion. Likewise, in the content areas, the students will plan, draft, fix, and finish projects, ranging from model airplanes to biography reports, while applying the Writing Process to whatever they do. By helping the students raise their awareness of this process, you can show them what to do physically when they sit down to write (as opposed to using the Traits of Good Writing to show them how to write well). The Writing Process provides the mechanics by which the students will complete writing-based content area assignments.

The Writing Process consists of the following steps. They are generally followed in this order, though the students may return to any step at any time in the process to make changes:

- Prewriting
- Drafting
- Revision
- Editing
- Publishing

Prewriting

Students organize their initial (brainstormed) thoughts using techniques such as lists, outlines, mind webs (bubbling), illustrations, or whatever assignment-specific technique is appropriate. Prewriting can also include researching, planning for special layout, designing hands-on construction, and any other organizing that takes place before the students dive into creating what will become a finished product.

Drafting

While drafting a traditional writing assignment, the students would transform the ideas of their prewrite into paragraph (or at least sentence) form. In the content areas, drafting may look the same, or could include sketching plans, writing excerpts that will later be included on a poster, building an initial model, etc. Drafting should not be published work; the students who strive for perfect drafts frequently get mired in mechanics and fail to successfully get their ideas on the page. Encourage the students to draft for ideas and organization, leaving work on perfection for later in the Writing Process.

The Writing Process *(cont.)*

Revision

Revision is not editing! In this step, the students will revise the content of their piece. The students should first revise their own work and may then use input from peers, parents, or from you. One tip in avoiding busywork is to have the students revise directly on their draft (without recopying a new draft). It is helpful to have a green pen or pencil to use for revision, which can help make the distinction between the red pencil you use (or have students use) to mark mistakes while editing.

Editing

In this step, the students will correct the mechanics of their writing and will likely need input from a peer-editing partner or from an adult. Spelling, punctuation, and grammar will be corrected during editing. It is helpful to have a red pen or pencil for editing; this helps the students differentiate between revision (green marks) and editing (red marks).

Publishing

In the content areas, publishing will take many forms, from the traditional paper to a Mars Lander mounted on cardboard with written descriptions of its features. Whatever the format, publishing should include attention to Presentation. You might want to create publishing norms for your class at the beginning of the year, displaying your criteria for a published paper where the students can reference them as needed. Depending on your preferences and classroom resources, you may require published work to be word processed, written in pen, include a certain format of name-date-class, be a specific font and size, etc.

Content-Area Adjustments to the Writing Process

In the content areas, you will not always be writing in the traditional sense of the word. As such, you might want to transform the Writing Process with the following guidelines in mind:

- With younger classes, most teachers choose to abbreviate the Writing Process in favor of overall assignments, rather than dwelling on each step.

- Many instances of content area writing will use only parts of the Writing Process (i.e., students would not necessarily revise notes they wrote during a lesson, and they may not share ideas they brainstorm as part of designing a hypothetical science experiment).

- As the primary goal of writing in the content areas is to reinforce information, not necessarily to develop writing style (this will be done during writing class), you may not ask the students to revise as thoroughly for Sentence Fluency and Conventions. In fact, you might not care if certain words are spelled correctly as long as the required information is present.

Learning Centers in the Content Areas

One format for class time that promotes content area writing is the learning center. Learning centers are areas of your room where small groups can work independently. You may have heard the term literacy center, which is a learning center that focuses on reading or writing. In the learning center classroom, you may have multiple projects going on at once through which the students will rotate, or you may have one project with different levels of difficulty. At a learning center, the students will find simple directions and all the materials they need to complete an activity. For example, a group of four students might complete a learning center in which they work together to make a simple model of the solar system and then collaborate to write about the planet on which they would most like to live. Learning centers can be especially useful in content area classes in which you assign hands-on projects. By including a writing component at the end of each learning center project, you can help ensure that the groups who finish early have something to do and the groups who need more time can catch up.

Setting up Learning Centers

If you choose to use learning centers in your class, you will need to set up the room, prepare the centers, and thoroughly explain your expectations to the students before starting. As much as possible, each center should be independent from the others. First, choose how many centers you want to be able to run at one time, and then do your best to create an area of the classroom devoted to each.

Keep the following in mind when setting up learning centers:

- Some learning centers require writing and craft materials. Consider setting up a central location where the students can access materials as needed.

- Use moveable furniture, hanging sheets or shower curtains, wooden lattice, or portable partitions to section your classroom into learning center areas.

- Label your learning centers, but make sure your labels do not define the center's level. For example, make sure your lowest group is not always in center number one. (You don't want the "number ones" feeling bad about their ability!)

- You might design one learning center to be used as a small-group instruction area where you can oversee more complex activities or offer remedial help.

- Vary your small groups so that the students work with a variety of peers, rather than stigmatizing low, middle, and high groups. Also consider putting a struggling student with a group of more able peers in hopes that this student will learn from the others.

Learning Centers in the Content Areas *(cont.)*

Setting Learning Center Expectations

The students will need to understand what you expect of them in the learning centers. A strong management strategy will allow your students to successfully complete independent centers and allow you to work with small groups of students during center time.

Consider the following when preparing the students for learning centers:

- Before starting learning centers, thoroughly explain and model the procedure. With less experienced classes, you will likely need to demonstrate the directions for each learning center. (In this case, consider running fewer centers at once.)
- For the first few learning centers, don't trap yourself in small-group instruction; rather, check in with each group to help solidify learning center procedure and behavior.
- Have a student model the procedure as you explain it.
- Choose sample small groups and practice going to and from learning centers.
- Review the materials that students will need for each learning center, and show the students where they can find the materials.
- Explain that cooperation is part of learning centers. In many learning centers, the students will need to work together to accomplish their goals. Review a center and ask a group of students to model how they might cooperate to complete it.

Assessing Learning Centers

Consider choosing from the following techniques to assess students' work during learning centers.

Anecdotal Records

If you are not instructing a small group or otherwise engaged during learning centers, walk around the room taking notes on student involvement. Keep these notes organized with each student's file and refer to them during parent conferences and meetings and when determining future groups. One useful strategy for organizing anecdotal records is to print students' names on sticky labels, write notes on these labels, and then later stick the corresponding label in each student's section of a notebook.

Assessing the Finished Product

Many learning centers include an assignment or task that the students will complete (whether it is a writing project or not). You can assess this finished product using the Traits of Good Writing or an appropriate rubric.

Self-Assessment

Develop a rubric and have the students grade themselves. For example, you might list criteria such as "labeled each planet" and "worked as a team," and have each student rank himself or herself from 1 to 5, listing one thing he or she did well and one thing he or she would like to do better next time.

Visual Feedback

At the end of the day, distribute stars or other small visual awards. For example, the students who did their best throughout the day may earn three stars, whereas the students who had difficulties participating during the activity might earn only one. You might choose to organize these on a class chart, with the students who reach a certain number of stars earning a reward.

Assessment of the Traits of Good Writing

One of the tools you will need in your bag of tricks is a rubric to evaluate students' writing. In this book, a different scoring rubric is included for each writing-based unit. You will find a scoring rubric on the last page of each unit. The Traits of Good Writing is one of the more popular rubrics for assessing a writing assignment and is flexible enough to apply to content area assignments, as well as to traditional writing work. Though the Traits are basically an assessment system, they can also be used for instruction and discussion.

Writing can be broken into its seven major Traits: Ideas, Organization, Voice, Word Choice, Sentence Fluency, Conventions, and Presentation. By assessing each Trait separately, we can give the students specific feedback and target certain areas for improvement.

The Traits of Good Writing can also be used to discuss what makes writing "good" or "bad," whether evaluating students' own writing or published work. By raising awareness of each Trait, the students will learn to recognize them in their own writing. In addition, they will have the proper language to describe and improve the quality of their writing.

When working with emergent writers, you can apply the Traits to illustrations and hands-on projects. For example, you could score Ideas based on the precise observations included in a student's illustration of an acorn; Voice could be seen in the personality of a clay figure.

The Traits Defined

Ideas

Ideas make up the content of a piece. In a subject area, Ideas refer to the information in a piece of writing—does it demonstrate an understanding of the desired material and present all the needed information? A main idea, or topic, should be supported by relevant accompanying details. Ideas interest and inform, excite, and entertain; in good writing, they define a thought perfectly while remaining precise and concise. When assessing for content understanding, you may weigh Ideas more heavily than the other Traits.

Ideas might be expressed by:

- a detailed drawing, showing unexpected observations that others might have missed
- any feature on the page that shows creativity and/or careful thought

Word Choice

In the content areas, Word Choice frequently refers to subject-specific vocabulary: Does a student demonstrate knowledge of the needed vocabulary? For example, instead of saying in a math word problem that numbers are *timesed*, a student would use the correct term, *multiplied*. Good Word Choice also concisely defines Ideas using words with precise meaning.

Word Choice might be expressed by:

- an attempt to use new words learned from listening, reading, or conversation

Sentence Fluency

Sentence Fluency in the content areas creates clarity and enhances meaning. Sentences flow without hesitation using a variety of constructions, creating an ever-changing rhythm that is easy to read aloud.

Sentence Fluency might be expressed by:

- adding *The* to the title *Spider* to create the heading of an illustration

The Traits Defined *(cont.)*

Voice

A content area piece with strong Voice demonstrates an author's passion for and command of the subject area. The writing should speak directly to the intended audience using an appropriate nonfiction tone (businesslike without being dry), creating a connection between the reader and the author.

Voice might be expressed by:

- color, energy, and individual style
- elements of the project that define the author's identity, even if the student has forgotten to write his or her name

Organization

The piece is constructed in a way that leads from an interesting opening to a thought-provoking conclusion without unnecessary digression. While pieces need not be predictable, they should have a logical framework, showing careful planning and foresight. Details are relevant to the section in which they are included and combine to support the topic or storyline.

Organization might be expressed by:

- a balance of art and text
- a layout that shows where things start and end (e.g., title, caption, illustration in a box)

Conventions

Does the student demonstrate a mastery of grade-appropriate grammar, punctuation, spelling, paragraphing, capitalization, etc.? Anything included in the mechanics of language falls into the category of Conventions.

Conventions might be expressed by:

- text that goes from left to right or is organized in lines
- punctuation marks, even if they are in the wrong place

Presentation

Strong Presentation offers information in a clear, visually appealing manner. Meaning is highlighted by layout, graphics, and neatness, and the reader immediately desires to give the piece a closer look. In the content areas, you will likely need to define what you expect in terms of Presentation and format for each assignment.

Presentation might be expressed by:

- ability to distinguish between what is writing and illustrations
- how the blank space is used on the page

Scoring Basics

- You will score each Trait separately from 1–5, with 1 being the lowest and 5 the highest.

- There is no need to assess every Trait on every assignment. Consider which Traits are applicable to each assignment and assess accordingly.

- Remember, in assessing emergent writers, you may be applying the Traits to drawings, conversations, and projects, as well as to writing.

- Always find something to praise!

Scoring Rubric for Writing Traits

	5	**3**	**1**
Ideas	The paper's central idea is clear, focused, and supported by vivid, relevant details.	The writer has defined a topic, but it is supported by few or mundane details.	The writer has not yet defined a topic; details are lacking or irrelevant. Writing may be scribbles.
Word Choice	The writer uses precise, natural, and engaging words to convey the intended message.	While the writer's meaning is clear, word choice lacks energy; words are functional but routine.	Words are used incorrectly or the writer uses such limited vocabulary that meaning is impaired.
Voice	The writer is obviously aware of the audience, communicating in an engaging and personal tone.	While functional, the voice is impersonal; the piece could have been written by anybody.	The writer seems indifferent to the audience or topic; the readers are unmoved and left flat.
Sentence Fluency	Sentences flow easily and are a pleasure to read aloud.	The text can be read aloud with practice.	The text cannot be read aloud. You can't guess the author's intent.
Organization	Organization is clear and obvious, including an introduction, body, and conclusion.	A motivated reader can find meaning, but the path is indirect.	There is no identifiable structure; events and information are random.
Conventions	Even complex conventions enhance meaning and readability. There are few errors.	The writer controls grade-appropriate conventions but struggles to use more complex conventions.	Errors make the piece difficult to read. The writer incorrectly uses basic conventions.
Presentation	Layout and presentation enhance meaning and visual appeal.	The piece is legible and neat, neither adding to nor detracting from meaning and appeal.	Presentation is distracting or messy, making meaning unclear.

Learning to Score the Traits

Your first attempts at assessing student work using the Traits of Good Writing will be slow. To increase the speed at which you become comfortable with the Traits, consider trying the following:

- Recruit a colleague as an assessment partner. Pick students' writing to study, and assess it independently. Once you have scored the writing without collaboration, compare your scores and discuss. There's a good chance you won't agree, and that's okay! This is a learning process in which you will both be exploring the nuances of the Traits. Discussion of your disparities in scores is as important, if not more important, as coming to a consensus on what number each Trait deserves. Neither of you will be "wrong," but by justifying your score, you will gain experience with the language of the Traits and the elements that make up each.

- Give yourself a little extra time at first. Don't jump into your first attempt at Trait-based scoring late on a Tuesday night, with 25 major assignments to grade by morning!

- Visit one of the following Web sites, which offer practice scoring, lessons, and information about the Traits of Good Writing.

Northwest Regional Educational Laboratory
http://www.nwrel.org
Oregon Public Education Network
http://www.openc.k12.or.us/scoring/getstart.php
Albuquerque Public Schools
http://www.aps.edu/aps/Cochiti/6traits/
Kent (Washington) School District
http://www.kent.k12.wa.us/staff/LindaJancola/6Trait/6-trait.html
Web English Teacher
http://www.webenglishteacher.com/6traits.html

Weighing the Traits to Fit Your Assignments

The basic total score of 35 works well when you ask the students to improve all areas of their writing equally (i.e., Word Choice is equally as important as Ideas or Conventions). However, in a content area assignment, one or more of the Traits might be more important than the others. For example, you may want more emphasis on Ideas, checking for comprehension and retention of subject area material. For an illustrated poster, you may weigh Presentation higher than the other Traits. This method has the advantage of accentuating the most important parts of the assignment while giving less weight to writing style. Use the Weighted Scoring Rubric on page 23 to emphasize the Trait(s) most important to you.

Teaching Using the Traits of Good Writing

While the basis of the Traits of Good Writing is an assessment rubric, you may also use the Traits to instruct in the following two ways.

Feedback Using the Assessment Data

Scoring each Trait allows you to give positive feedback to the students on their areas of strength, allowing them to feel successful while pinpointing the area(s) in which they could improve. Noticing the lowest-scoring Trait on a given assignment, the teacher might ask the student to take special care with this Trait on the next project, or might provide the student with extra practice on specific Traits. Scoring the Traits will also help you gauge general class levels. For example, you might notice that your class's use of Word Choice lags behind other scores. In this case, you might choose to target the class with a Word Choice lesson during the time in your day devoted to writing instruction, or you might choose to focus more on important vocabulary terms in the next unit of study.

Using the Language of the Traits

Writing experts, such as Ralph Fletcher, recommend that teachers and students regularly analyze and critique the work of other authors and writers.

In the content areas, you might discuss the Organization of a science magazine article or the Sentence Fluency of a math word problem. There will be many opportunities to discuss authors' uses of Ideas as you evaluate the content of assigned readings. You may also use the Traits to compare and contrast different content area writing.

By analyzing sample readings using the Traits of Good Writing, the students will learn the characteristics of good writing and, as a result, will be better able to transfer these skills to their own writing. The more you use the language of the Traits in your classroom, the more aware the students will become of the Traits in their own writing.

Weighted Scoring Rubric

	5	3	1	Points	Weight	Total
Ideas	The paper's central idea is clear, focused, and supported by vivid, relevant details.	The writer has defined a topic, but it is supported by few or mundane details.	The writer has not yet defined a topic; details are lacking or irrelevant. Writing may be scribbles.			
Word Choice	The writer uses precise, natural, and engaging words to convey the intended message.	While the writer's meaning is clear, word choice lacks energy; words are functional but routine.	Words are used incorrectly or the writer uses such limited vocabulary that meaning is impaired.			
Voice	The writer is obviously aware of the audience, communicating in an engaging and personal tone.	While functional, the voice is impersonal; the piece could have been written by anybody.	The writer seems indifferent to the audience or topic; the readers are unmoved and left flat.			
Sentence Fluency	Sentences flow easily and are a pleasure to read aloud.	The text can be read aloud with practice.	The text cannot be read aloud. You can't guess the author's intent			
Organization	Organization is clear and obvious, including an introduction, body, and conclusion.	A motivated reader can find meaning, but the path is indirect.	There is no identifiable structure; events and information are random.			
Conventions	Even complex conventions enhance meaning and readability. There are few errors.	The writer controls grade-appropriate conventions but struggles to use more complex conventions.	Errors make the piece difficult to read. The writer incorrectly uses basic conventions.			
Presentation	Layout and presentation enhance meaning and visual appeal.	The piece is legible and neat, neither adding to nor detracting from meaning and appeal.	Presentation is distracting or messy, making meaning unclear.			
Total Points Possible (sum of "weight" column, times 5)						**Total Points Earned**

Example Use of Weighted Scoring Rubric

Assignment: Poster describing the effects of pollution on the environment

	5	3	1	Points	Weight	Total
Ideas	The paper's central idea is clear, focused, and supported by vivid, relevant details.	The writer has defined a topic, but it is supported by few or mundane details.	The writer has not yet defined a topic; details are lacking or irrelevant. Writing may be scribbles.	4	5	20
Word Choice	The writer uses precise, natural, and engaging words to convey the intended message.	While the writer's meaning is clear, word choice lacks energy; words are functional but routine.	Words are used incorrectly or the writer uses such limited vocabulary that meaning is impaired.	3.5	2	7
Voice	The writer is obviously aware of the audience, communicating in an engaging and personal tone.	While functional, the voice is impersonal; the piece could have been written by anybody.	The writer seems indifferent to the audience or topic; the readers are unmoved and left flat.	3	1	3
Sentence Fluency	Sentences flow easily and are a pleasure to read aloud.	The text can be read aloud with practice.	The text cannot be read aloud. You can't guess the author's intent	3	2	6
Organization	Organization is clear and obvious, including an introduction, body, and conclusion.	A motivated reader can find meaning, but the path is indirect.	There is no identifiable structure; events and information are random.	3.5	1	3.5
Conventions	Even complex conventions enhance meaning and readability. There are few errors.	The writer controls grade-appropriate conventions but struggles to use more complex conventions.	Errors make the piece difficult to read. The writer incorrectly uses basic conventions.	2.5	2	5
Presentation	Layout and presentation enhance meaning and visual appeal.	The piece is legible and neat, neither adding to nor detracting from meaning and appeal.	Presentation is distracting or messy, making meaning unclear.	4	4	16
Total Points Possible (sum of "weight" column, times 5)						**Total Points Earned** 60.5

Implementing Writing-Based Lessons in Your Classroom

Now that you have refreshed the writing teacher's bag of tricks, you are ready to help the students apply these techniques in your content area classroom. Unfortunately, it's not as easy as simply saying, "Use the Writing Process, consider adding Learning Centers, and don't forget about the Traits of Good Writing!" The students need to be scaffolded into the process; fortunately you can do so while teaching your content area material.

In this section we will look at the following:

- demonstrating strong finished products through reading published work in the same format/genre/content area as the assignment

- helping the students get started by modeling the process for Written Assignments (a step-by-step reference for your first writing-based content area assignment)

- giving the students a clear picture of how to go about Written Assignments for the remainder of the year (a reference for continuing writing-based content area assignments)

Step 1: Modeling Content Area Writing through Textbook Reading and Beyond

The most powerful tools you can give the students when asking them to write in a content area are examples of the type of writing you expect. For example, before having the students write about a current science event, have them read excerpts from science magazines such as *Kids Discover*. When looking at writing examples, reread them more than once. Show the students how to look at writing examples as writers, not as readers. While analyzing model material, have the students discuss not only the content, but also the style of the writing. Here are a few teaching strategies for looking at writing models:

- The students list one thing the author of the example did well in each of the seven Traits of Good Writing (e.g., Ideas: Tadpoles are baby frogs; Organization: the author started by describing a pond by his house; Sentence Fluency: frogs lay eggs in a huge clump, which looks like tapioca pudding; Word Choice: tadpole, salamander; Presentation: I loved the close-up pictures of tadpole eyes).

- The students find one sentence they find boring and offer suggestions for its revision.

- Discuss the organization of the example and ask the students to create a chart describing the overall format scheme.

- Have the students summarize the sample in writing.

In addition to your textbook and content area picture books, the following magazines are resources for modeling writing in the content areas:

Science

Ranger Rick (or *Ranger Rick's NatureScope*)

National Geographic for Kids

Chirp (or *chickaDEE* or *OWL*)

Click

Cricket (or *Ladybug* or *Spider*)

Kids Discover

Your Big Backyard

Odyssey: Adventures in Science

Science and Children

Wild Outdoor World

Wonder Science

Math

Scholastic DynaMath

Scholastic MATH

Mathematics Magazine (grades 1–12)

Social Studies

Appleseeds

Cobblestone

Time for Kids

National Geographic Kids (ages 8–14)

World and I

World Kid Magazine

History for Kids

Faces: People, Places, and Cultures

Footsteps Magazine

Skipping Stones

Health

Jack and Jill

U.S. Kids

Step 2: Modeled and Shared Writing Experiences

In the first writing assignment of the year, the students will need to learn the mechanics of the Writing Process, if they don't know them already. Simply explaining the steps is not enough and will lead to a deluge of questions during the assignment. To scaffold your students into independent work, you will need to model the process. Even if your students claim they already know it, you should still model the process so they better understand your expectations.

For your students' first assignment, assign a fun, short topic. An upcoming holiday topic usually works well. First, model it by writing your own paper in front of the class, demonstrating each step. You may want to demonstrate one step of the Writing Process each day, following the lesson with independent work time during which the students will use the same step in their own writing. After your students are comfortable with the process of how writing looks in your classroom, then allow them to choose their own topics.

If your class seems unsure or has significant difficulties with the writing included in the first assignment, you may want to include another demonstration during the next project. This time, instead of simply modeling the Writing Process, allow each student to write with you, creating a sample product with the class's input. Obviously, the students will be quicker at this process if you are also using the Writing Process in your language arts class.

Step 3: Tips for Managing Later Assignments

In your writing-based content area lessons throughout the year, keep the following in mind:

- Continue to help the students visualize a strong final product through reading relevant samples before allowing the students to prewrite their own projects.

- If at all possible, score even hands-on projects, visual presentations, journals, or small daily assignments using the Traits of Good Writing. Remember—you don't need to score all seven Traits every time!

- The students should have the opportunity to share their finished work. If possible, writing with real-world purpose (e.g., letter to the editor of the local paper or article submitted to a kid's magazine) will demonstrate the reasons why the students should care about improving their writing.

- Consider having an Author's Chair, a special seat in which the students share aloud their work with the class. This activity helps to ensure that the students put forward their best effort. Listeners should be encouraged to tell what writing Trait they think was done well, which gives positive reinforcement to authors.

- The more you integrate your language arts class with your content area classes, using the language of the Traits of Good Writing and the mechanics of the Writing Process across curricular areas, the more comfortable your students will become with these techniques.

Writing Minilessons for the Content Areas

Every teacher occasionally has free time at the beginning or end of a class period. What better way to use that time than with a writing minilesson? This chapter features short lessons to start or end a period, although they can also be used as daily warm-ups or once a week on a designated day.

If you choose to use these lessons frequently, consider asking the students to keep a content area writing journal in which they will organize all their responses. (You might have them divide their journals into a section for each subject.) This allows you to periodically collect and assess a number of assignments without needing to keep track of reams of loose paper. Depending on the weight you give each assignment, you might choose to assess journals based solely on volume or use the Traits of Good Writing to assess a number of assignments together (i.e., assess an entire month as one assignment, giving relevant feedback using the Traits).

If you're using the Traits to assess writing journals, review with the students the specific rubric you will use when scoring (see page 24 for an example) so that the students know what you are expecting. For example, you might choose to weigh Ideas more heavily than Conventions, as you will likely not be allowing time for revision and editing. Perhaps your rubric will add criteria for volume, allowing you to assess for thorough completion. You may want to weigh Presentation lower in comparison to other Traits or not assess it at all.

Whichever format and assessment method you choose, the majority of these daily writing ideas are meant to be fun. While you will collect and assess responses, you should encourage the students to write their thoughts without fear of being labeled "wrong." These journals are meant to be somewhere between the free-writing journals of a fiction class and a traditional science lab notebook. Allow the students to "write their minds"!

Minilessons: Writing to Prompts

A writing prompt has two basic components: the prompt itself and directions explaining what the students should do with it. Not only can writing to prompts encourage the students to think about a content area, but it can also prepare them for the format of many standardized tests. In this way, you can teach to the test without compromising instruction. At the time of this book's publication, the following Web sites were useful sources of content area writing prompts:

- **General Writing Prompts**

  http://www.canteach.ca/elementary/prompts.html

- **Science Writing Prompts (organized by grade level)**

  http://home.wsd.wednet.edu/WSD/learnteach/writingprompts.htm

- **Expository Writing Prompts (formatted on reproducible sheets)**

  http://www.manatee.k12.fl.us/sites/elementary/palmasola/wexpository.htm

Descriptive Writing to Visual Prompts (Using Sensory Details)

Choose a photograph, poster, or picture from the desired subject area such as a battle scene from the Civil War or an electronics assembly line in Tokyo. Many textbook publishers have illustrations that supplement their books and materials for this purpose. Ask the students to visualize themselves in the picture. What would they see, hear, taste, touch, or smell? What would they experience if they were in the picture? Even in math class, you can use pictures, including graphs, charts, M.C. Escher paintings, pictures of fractals, and other "math art."

Writing Responses to Thought-Provoking Questions

Depending on the subject area, you might ask the students to periodically reflect on the material through written responses to thought-provoking questions. Successful thought questions frequently ask the students their opinion about an issue for which the subject material has provided background information. For example, during science class, you might ask the students to write their opinions about controversial topics such as whether space travel is worth the money. With emergent writers, you can have them draw a "what if" scene and label pieces of it.

Minilessons: Writing to Prompts *(cont.)*

Lead Sentence Writing

Give the students a short sentence meant to spark their memory, and then ask them to extend this thinking. The following are examples of lead sentence prompts:

- In an ecosystem, everything works together. One example of this is . . . .

- The first president of the United States was George Washington. He . . . .

- Two and 12 are factors of 24. Other factors of 24 are . . . .

- Eating fruits and vegetables helps guard against getting sick. A healthful diet is also important because . . . .

Completion

Much like lead sentence writing, completion asks the students to use their thoughts to extend an unfinished prompt. The following are examples of completion prompts:

- Three, 7, 11, and 15 are all odd numbers because . . . .

- Abraham Lincoln was the country's most important president because . . . .

- The strangest thing I noticed in the stream was . . . .

- The most important thing to remember when planning a healthful meal is . . . .

Scaffolding Questions

You probably already write tests with the most difficult questions at the end. Use scaffolded prompts in the same way to lead the students toward higher levels of thinking. The following is an example of scaffolded questions: "What are the three body sections of an insect and how many legs do they have? What are the two body sections of an arachnid and how many legs do they have? How are insects different from arachnids?"

Minilessons: Responding to Reading

As discussed earlier, it is difficult to separate content area writing from content area reading, and why would you want to? After reading articles, textbook excerpts, picture books, or other informational material, it is natural to have the students respond in writing. Consider using one of the following techniques to help focus your students' thoughts.

Paraphrasing and Summarizing

Paraphrasing and summarizing can be useful tools when simply checking for comprehension of reading material. Always encourage the students to use their own words when describing an assigned reading to avoid having the students copying without understanding. Show the students how to paraphrase and summarize by modeling a few examples. Also explain about plagiarism so the students will know to avoid it!

Cued Retelling

Especially with less experienced classes, you might want to revisit reading material in a class discussion before asking the students to write about it (or paraphrase it). In cued retelling, you can have the students raise their hands to offer the things they remember from the text. With the class collaborating, try to remember every detail of the reading.

Reading Response Journals

Having the students respond to something they've already read is an excellent way to apply content area writing.

After reading in your content area, encourage the students to make connections with the text in the form of reading response journals. Here are some sample questions that students may answer:

- What does this reading make you think of? Do you have any personal examples?

- What else have you read that relates to this reading?

- What is one thing that you found especially interesting?

- What is one question you have after the reading?

Learning Logs

Learning logs are a combination of a reading response journal and a book of organized class notes. You might have the students make a short entry in their learning log after every time they read from a textbook, writing down one thing they learned. You can encourage your class to think of their learning logs as a record of things that go into their brains. At the end of the year, they might be surprised at what they know!

Additional Writing Minilessons

Word-Bank Writing (Using Content Area Vocabulary)

Write on the board some or all of the vocabulary learned in a unit. The students will use this vocabulary while writing in any format you choose. Consider having the students draw a scene using the vocabulary and then label the drawing.

Reflective Writing

After teaching, you can ask the students to reflect on the lesson in writing using the same questions as those used for Reading Response Journals, or you might use "What, So What, Now What" questions like the following:

- What did you learn in this lesson?

- How does this apply to what we have been studying?

- What questions do you have that you would like answered in future learning experiences?

Focused Free Writing (10–15 minutes of nonstop writing)

Encourage the students to write as much as they can in a short period of time. Focused Free Writing works well at the end of units or after the students have learned significant background information about a subject. To set the mood, you might ask your class to visualize the subject about which they will be free writing (or quickly illustrate it). Once the activity starts, the students should write everything they know about the topic. Some teachers play soft music during writing time. During Focused Free Writing, the students should not get up to use the restroom, sharpen pencils, etc., as such disruptions are distracting to others. Make sure the students have had a break before you begin. Ask them simply to write for volume! When assessing Focused Free Writing, you will want to weigh Ideas over Traits such as Conventions and Presentation. Encourage emergent writers to illustrate their writing, or reduce the amount of time allotted to Focused Free Writing.

Graphic Organizers

Either distribute one of the organizers from this book (see pages 89–96), or have the students create their own graphic organizer in which they display information from a selected reading. One successful strategy is to first use existing graphic organizers, working toward a level of familiarity that allows the students to later create their own.

Oral Prewriting

With a less confident class, consider using discussion as a form of prewriting before asking the students to write on their own. For example, you might talk about what the students observed during a zoo fieldtrip before asking them to illustrate and label a picture of what they saw. Likewise, you might have the students tell you the sequence of events in a book before putting their thoughts on paper. You can even pair the students and have them tell their ideas to each other, as the primary benefit of this activity is in simply offering the author a sounding board before he or she starts to write.

Ready-to-Use Activities

Use the following high-impact lessons to spice up your content area classes while encouraging your students to practice and improve their writing skills.

As all lessons include a writing component, the National Writing Standards met by each lesson are referenced in the "Standards of Writing" (see pages 6–7). Additional content area standards are listed individually.

Chain of Life

Overview

Students will brainstorm items of different sizes (from a molecule to the universe), write the items on provided strips, and then work to order these strips from smallest to largest. At the end of this activity, the students will staple together the strips to form a chain of life, with each student included as an important link.

Subjects	Writing, Science
Materials	• Colored pens or pencils • Stapler • "How Big?" (page 37), "Thing Strips" (pages 38–39), "Blank Thing Strips" (page 40), "People Strips" (page 41), and "Grading Rubric: Chain of Life" (page 42)
Time	At least two 50-minute periods
Preparation	1. Make one copy per group of "Thing Strips" (pages 38–39), "Blank Thing Strips" (page 40), and "Blank People Strips" (page 41). Cut out the strips. 2. Make one copy per group of "How Big?" (page 37). 3. Make one copy of "Grading Rubric: Chain of Life" (page 42) for each student.
Written Assignment: Word slips (page 40) to create a Chain of Life	

Objectives

As a result of this activity, the students will:

* gain an overview of their place in the universe
* cooperate as a class to create a finished product
* practice their brainstorming skills

Standards

Writing

1–E, F, G; 2–A; 5–A, B, C, F

Science

As a result of activities in grades K–4, all students should develop an understanding of:

* objects in the sky

Chain of Life *(cont.)*

Lesson Opening

1. Ask the students, "What is the smallest thing you can think of?" When they answer, ask them to think of something smaller than that. Explain that there are things even smaller than a grain of sand—so small that you can't even see them!

2. Ask the students, "What is the biggest thing you can think of?" Then ask them, "What is bigger than that?"

3. Explain that compared to a grain of sand, you would imagine that a student feels rather big, but compared to an elephant, a student might feel small. Compared to the planet or the solar system or the universe, it's easy to feel really small!

4. If desired, take the students outside and have them look at the sky (but not at the sun!). Have the students tell you what they see. Ask them, "What is past the clouds? What is past the blue sky? What is past the planets, and even past that? What is past the edges of the universe?"

Lesson Directions

1. Tell the students that they will be completing an activity that will help them decide how big they are. Divide the students into groups of four.

2. Review with the students the "How Big?" (page 37) sheet and explain the following procedure:
   - A student from each group will choose three Thing Strips.
   - The group will write these items on the "How Big?" (page 37) sheet in order, from smallest to biggest. (Demonstrate this process for your students.)
   - Once they have ordered their Thing Strips, the group will brainstorm four more items to write on this sheet—one item that is smaller than anything on their sheet, one that is between each pair of things on their sheet, and one that is bigger than anything listed. Model this procedure for your students.
   - Ask the students to be careful with the strips because you will need them later in the activity.

3. Once a group shows you a completed "How Big?" (page 37) sheet, give them four Blank Thing Strips and ask them to write and illustrate each of the four items they brainstormed (one per strip).

4. Now comes the difficult part! In your class, you should have many strips—those provided in this book and those that groups illustrated—have your class put all the strips in order, keeping the following in mind:
   - In the spirit of a teambuilding challenge, it is desirable for the students to organize themselves independently to order their strips—of course, complete independence is likely impossible and you should give your class enough direction to avoid chaos!
   - One successful strategy is to have each student be responsible for a few strips. Create a size line that runs across one wall of your classroom, with markers such as mouse, person, elephant, and country creating reference points. Have the students set their strips in the correct place and then make revisions with the class as necessary.

Chain of Life *(cont.)*

Lesson Directions *(cont.)*

5. Once the strips are organized, gather them in a pile, taking care to keep them in order!

6. Now explain that you need to add each student to this pile of items. Give each student a Blank People Strip. Have the student write his or her name on the strip and illustrate it so that it looks like him or her.

7. Explain to the students that compared to the other objects they are ordering, the students are basically the same size.

8. Have the class help you lay out the strips (Thing and People Strips) in order.

9. Use a stapler to link the strips of this lesson into one long chain.

Lesson Closing

1. Display the completed chain in the classroom.

2. Where are your students in this chain? Does your class think there are more things in the world that are bigger than them, or more things that are smaller?

3. Do they think this chain is an accurate representation of how big/small they are in the universe? You might offer that there are millions and millions of grains of sand, but only one universe. Does this mean that the students are fairly large in the overall big/small scheme of things?

4. At the end of this activity, have each student draw a picture of himself or herself in the universe. Ask the students to include (with labels) at least five items from this lesson.

Written Assignment

Groups will collaborate to write and illustrate Thing Strips (page 40), and each student will draw and label a picture of himself or herself within the framework of the universe.

Chain of Life *(cont.)*

Names _____ Date _____

How Big?

Directions: Order your Thing Strips from smallest to biggest. Write the smallest Thing Strip on line 1 and the biggest one on line 3. Then write something on each line that is between the two things, smallest of all, or biggest of all.

A. (smallest item) _____

1. _____

B. (size between 1 and 2) _____

2. _____

C. (size between 2 and 3) _____

3. _____

D. (biggest item) _____

Chain of Life *(cont.)*

Name: _____ Date: _____

Thing Strips

	flea		
	board game		
	adult		
	car		

Chain of Life *(cont.)*

Name: _____ **Date:** _____

Thing Strips *(cont.)*

	New York City	
	United States	
	Earth	
	Solar System	

Chain of Life *(cont.)*

Name: _____**Date:**_____

Blank Thing Strips

	Thing	Illustration	
	Thing	Illustration	
	Thing	Illustration	
	Thing	Illustration	

Chain of Life *(cont.)*

Name: _____ **Date:** _____

Blank People Strips

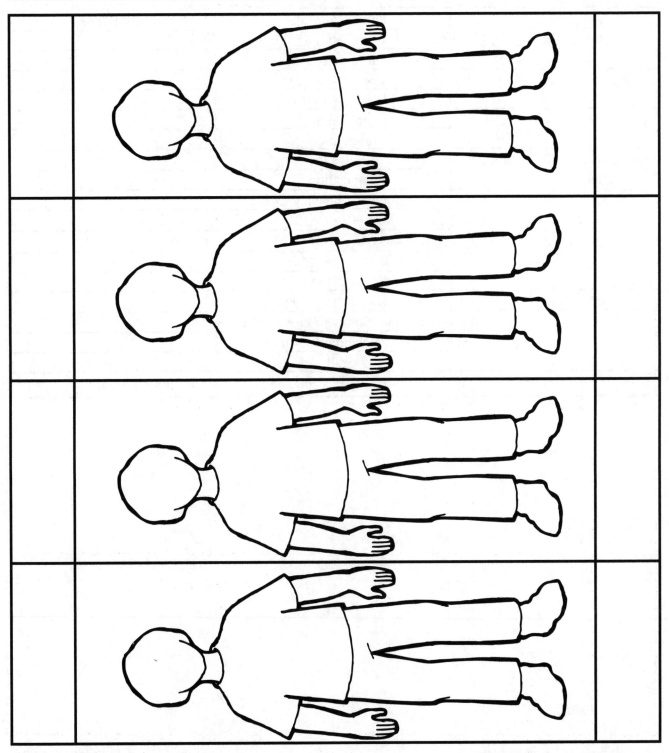

Chain of Life *(cont.)*

Grading Rubric: Chain of Life		
Name		**Date**
Assignment	**Points Possible**	**Points Earned**
"How Big" (page 37)	Completion (5)	
	Throughness (5)	
Thing Illustrations	Completion (5)	
	Presentation (5)	
Person Illustration	Completion (5)	
	Presentation (5)	
Universe and Me Illustration with labels	Voice (5)	
	Organization (5)	
	Sentence Fluency (5)	
	Word Choice (25)	
	Ideas (5)	
	Conventions (5)	
	Presentation (5)	
Participation	Cooperation during ordering (5)	
	Cooperation with group (5)	
	During chain creation (5)	
	Overall (5)	
	Total Points Possible: 85	**Points Earned:**

Picture Window Stories

Overview

Students will use magazine pictures to create translucent window stickers and then use them to spark ideas for short stories.

Subjects	Writing, Art
Materials	* One sheet of clear contact paper with backing (8.5" x 11" [21.3 x 28 cm]) for each student * Tub of water (e.g., small aluminum baking dish) for each student * Plastic spoons or rulers * Construction paper, writing paper, and scissors * Colored pens or pencils * Magazines with colorful pictures * A large window (or sheet of Plexiglas®) to display stickers * "Grading Rubric: Picture Window Stories" (page 46)
Time	Three 50-minute periods
Preparation	1. Section off an area of your room and place the tubs of water in that area. 2. Make one copy of "Grading Rubric: Picture Window Stories" (page 46) for each student.
Written Assignment: Illustration and short story, using art images as prompts	

Objectives

As a result of this activity, the students will:

- use art techniques to create novel window hangings
- use the Writing Process to create short, illustrated stories

Standards
Writing

1–A, B, C, F; 3–All; 5–A, C

Art

K–4: Knows how subject matter, symbols, and ideas are used to communicate meaning.

Picture Window Stories *(cont.)*

Lesson Opening

1. There are two parts to this activity: creating colorful window hangings and writing about them. The Lesson Opening section describes the art activity; the Lesson Directions section (see below) describes the writing.

2. To create translucent window pictures, the students will:

• Look through the magazines until they find a desired picture. Cut out this picture and place it on a desk or another smooth, hard surface.

• Pull off the contact-paper backing and place the sticky side down on the magazine picture.

• Rub the contact paper with a ruler or spoon to make sure it is *completely* stuck to the magazine image.

• Soak the picture and contact paper in water for at least 30 minutes—the contact paper glue will retain the ink from the picture.

• Lift the contact paper out of the tub and, under running water, gently rub off any paper fuzz that sticks to the contact paper.

• Set the picture aside to dry.

• If desired, create a frame for the picture using construction paper and colored pencils or pens.

• Tape the contact paper picture to the window. The light will shine through, creating a stained-glass effect!

Lesson Directions

1. Have your class sit directly in front of the collection of translucent window images. Turn off the lights to better appreciate students' artwork.

2. Admire the diversity of images—you might have lions and race cars, raccoons and ballerinas, or sports figures and cheesecake.

3. Ask the students what would happen if two of these unrelated images were in the same story? What would they do together? Give the students time to think about this.

Picture Window Stories *(cont.)*

Lesson Directions *(cont.)*

4. Explain that each image by itself suggests an obvious story, but you might have to be creative to write a story using more than one of these images. Make up your own short story using two or more of these images and tell it to the class—don't be afraid to be goofy! The story you create doesn't need to be perfect, but it should be an example of how you can bring two diverse ideas together.

5. Have your class work as a group to brainstorm possible stories, using two or more of the images on the window.

6. Explain that thinking about what you are going to write is an important step in the Writing Process—have each student think about a story that includes two or more window images.

7. Have the students illustrate this story and, under the illustration, write the story in a few sentences (requirements may differ, depending on the skills of you class). Explain that this step is called Drafting.

8. Give the students time to revise their story or add details to the illustration.

Lesson Closing

1. Encourage the students to present their stories to the class. Have each student point out the window pictures he or she used, display his or her illustration, and read his or her story.

2. Have the class offer compliments—what specifically did they like about each story?

3. If desired, as a group brainstorm ideas for combining two or more of your students' stories. Show that anything is possible in fiction if you use creativity!

Written Assignment

Each student will use the Writing Process to illustrate, title, and write a short story, based on translucent window pictures the students create.

Picture Windo Stories *(cont.)*

Grading Rubric: Picture Window Stories

Name _____ Date _____

Assignment	Points Possible	Points Earned
Translucent Window Coverage Art Project	Presentation (5)	
	Effort (5)	
Picture Window Story	Voice (5)	
	Organization (5)	
	Sentence Fluency (5)	
	Word Choice (5)	
	Ideas (5)	
	Conventions (5)	
	Presentation (5)	
Participation in Activity	(25)	
	Total Points Possible: 100	**Points Earned:**

Grading Rubric: Picture Window Stories

Name _____ Date _____

Assignment	Points Possible	Points Earned
Translucent Window Coverage Art Project	Presentation (5)	
	Effort (5)	
Picture Window Story	Voice (5)	
	Organization (5)	
	Sentence Fluency (5)	
	Word Choice (5)	
	Ideas (5)	
	Conventions (5)	
	Presentation (5)	
Participation in Activity	(25)	
	Total Points Possible: 100	**Points Earned:**

Toyland

Overview

Students will explore where a favorite toy is made, locating the country of origin on a world map and using reference materials to discover three facts about this place. Finally, the students will present their toy and location to the class.

Subjects	Writing, Geography
Materials	• Writing and illustrating supplies • Age-appropriate reference materials including the Internet, school library, basic encyclopedias (see books listed in Lesson Directions on page 48) • A large world map or set of atlases • "Toyland" (page 50) and "Grading Rubric: Toyland" (page 51)
Time	At least three 50-minute periods
Preparation	1. Make one copy of "Toyland" (page 50) and "Grading Rubric: Toyland" (page 51) for each student. 2. Make a chart with each student's name and a space for his or her country.

Written Assignment: Toyland Poster

Objectives

As a result of this activity, the students will:

• connect objects from their lives to places around the world
• use reference materials to find information about a country

Standards
Writing
1–A, G; 3–All; 4–A, B; 5–A, B, C, E, F

Geography

As a result of activities in grades K–12, all students should develop an understanding of:

• how to use maps and other geographic representations
• the physical and human characteristics of places
• how culture and experience influence people's perceptions of places and regions
• the patterns and networks of economic interdependence on Earth's surface

Toyland *(cont.)*

Lesson Opening

1. Starting at least three days before the first activity day, ask the students to look at their toys (at home) and find where one of these toys is made; if they can find a toy manufactured outside the United States, this will work best. Using a classroom toy, demonstrate how to find the "Made in _____" label. At the beginning of the class periods leading up to this activity, ask the students to tell you the places they found and write their country next to their names on a chart.

2. Make sure to provide toys for any students who have difficulty remembering to bring in a country or may not have toys available at home.

3. Ask the students *not* to bring these toys to class yet. However, let them know that at the end of the activity, they will be able to do so.

Lesson Directions

1. At the beginning of this activity, a country should be written next to every student's name on a class list.

2. Tell the students that before they can present their toy to the class, they will need to find three facts about the country where the toy was made. They will also be making a poster that tells the rest of the class about this country.

3. Distribute and review with the students "Toyland" (page 50).

4. The first step in completing this sheet is for each student to locate his or her toy's country of origin and to mark it on the map. Show the students the map resources they may use, and encourage the students to search these maps for their country, offering hints as needed. Many of their toys will be manufactured in Asian countries, so you might point out this part of the world.

48

Toyland *(cont.)*

Lesson Directions *(cont.)*

5. Once the students have marked their toy's country of origin, review the reference materials you will ask them to use to find three facts about this country. Have them record the facts on the "Toyland" (page 50) sheet. In addition to the Internet, basic encyclopedias, and the school library, the following are grade-appropriate sources of country knowledge:

   - *Afghanistan to Zimbabwe: Country Facts That Helped Me Win the National Geography Bee* by Andrew Wojtanik (National Geographic Children's Books, 2005)
   - *The Blackbirch Kid's Visual Reference of the World* (Blackbirch Press, 2001)
   - *Children from Australia to Zimbabwe: A Photographic Journey Around the World* by Marian Wright Edelman (Shakti for Children, 2001)

6. The students will now create posters that contain the following:
   - descriptive title
   - world map (from page 50) with their country marked
   - illustrations of the three facts they found
   - written descriptions of the three facts they found
   - decorations

7. Show the students the poster-making materials you want them to use and give them time to complete the project.

Lesson Closing

1. Have each student present his or her country to the class. You will likely have duplicate presentations on the same country—this is fine! You might even have the students who chose the same country present back to back, comparing the facts they found, or you might have these students work as a group to create one presentation.

2. Discuss the facts the students found and compare these countries to the United States. What similarities and/or differences did the students find?

3. If desired, discuss why many toys are not manufactured in the United States. Help the students understand what creates differing pay rates in different countries. Discuss working conditions around the world: Do the students think this is fair? What would these world communities do without manufacturing jobs? Obviously, this can be a difficult discussion (especially at this grade level), and one that you can explore in as much or as little depth as time allows.

Written Assignment

Each student will create a poster showing where his or her toy was manufactored and three captioned illustrations with research facts discovered about this country.

Toyland *(cont.)*

Name_____ Date _____

Toyland

Directions: Answer the questions. Use this information and the map and instructions below to create your Toyland Poster.

1. Where was your toy made? _____

2. Mark this country on the map below. _____

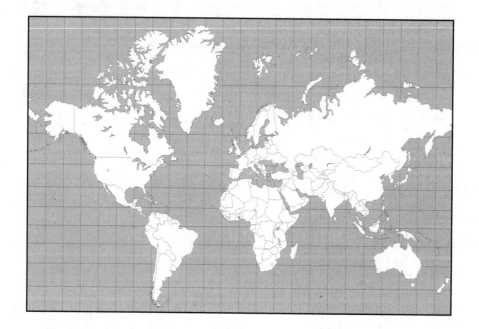

3. Write three facts about this country: _____

A. _____

B. _____

C. _____

On your poster, you should:

- Write a title.
- Include the map shown above.
- Mark your country.
- Write three facts.
- Draw your three facts.
- Add decorations as desired.

Toyland *(cont.)*

Grading Rubric: Toyland

Name _____ **Date** _____

Assignment	Points Possible	Points Earned
Toyland	Completion (10)	
	Three Researched Facts (15)	
Toyland Poster	Voice (5)	
	Organization (5)	
	Sentence Fluency (5)	
	Word Choice (5)	
	Ideas (5)	
	Conventions (5)	
	Presentation (5)	
Oral Presentation	Preperation (25)	
	Delivery (10)	
Participation in Activity	(20)	
	Total Points Possible: 100	**Points Earned:**

Grading Rubric: Toyland

Name _____ **Date** _____

Assignment	Points Possible	Points Earned
Toyland	Completion (10)	
	Three Researched Facts (15)	
Toyland Poster	Voice (5)	
	Organization (5)	
	Sentence Fluency (5)	
	Word Choice (5)	
	Ideas (5)	
	Conventions (5)	
	Presentation (5)	
Oral Presentation	Preperation (25)	
	Delivery (10)	
Participation in Activity	(20)	
	Total Points Possible: 100	**Points Earned:**

Bar Graphs

Overview

Students will write their names on sticky notes and post them in the form of bar graphs to chart various characteristics of students in their class.

Subjects	Writing, Math
Materials	• Colored pens • Overhead projector and transparency • "Graph" (page 55), "Bar Graphs" (page 56), and "Grading Rubric: Bar Graphs" (page 57)
Time	Two 50-minutes periods
Preparation	1. Draw a large graph on the board, suitable for use with the Lesson Opening (see page 53). 2. Copy "Graph" (page 55) onto a transparency. 3. Make one copy per group of "Bar Graphs" (page 56). 4. Make one copy of "Grading Rubric: Bar Graphs" (page 57) for each student.
Written Assignment: Bar Graphs (page 56)	

Objectives

As a result of this activity, the students will:

- explore the format of a bar graph
- learn to represent information on a bar graph

Standards

Writing

1–A, E, G; 4–A, B; 5–A, B, C, E, F

Math

As a result of activities in grades K–2, all students should:

- develop a sense of whole numbers and represent and use them in flexible ways
- connect number words and numerals to the quantities they represent, using various physical models and representations

Bar Graphs *(cont.)*

Lesson Opening

1. Tell the students that when looking at a group of numbers, it's sometimes difficult to know what they mean. For example, if someone looked at the class and said that six kids had brown hair, four had blond hair, nine had black hair, and two had red hair, you might start to get mixed up quickly: What was the most common hair color? Can you remember how many students had blond hair?

2. Ask the class if they have ever heard the phrase, "A picture is worth a thousand words." Tell them this can also be true with numbers. A picture that you make using numbers is called a graph. Graphs can make numbers easier to understand.

3. Explain that you are going to work together to graph the students' hair colors (or other characteristic such as which season has the most birthdays). Give each student one sticky note and have the student write his or her name on this note in big letters. While the students are writing, write the following categories along the bottom of the graph on the board: brown, blond, red, black.

4. Have the students come to the board, one at a time, to place their sticky note in the appropriate category, forming a bar graph as shown below:

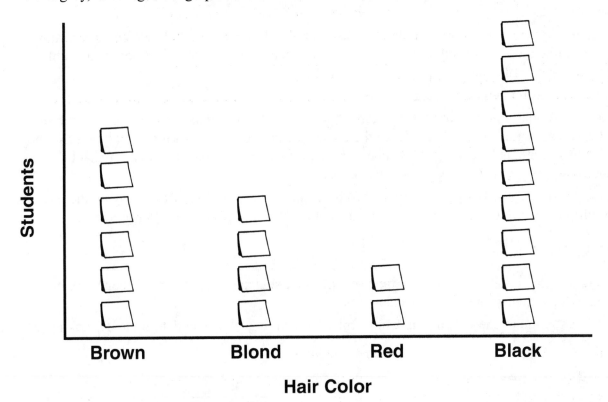

5. Now ask the students what information they can get from this graph. Is it easy to tell which category has the most? Can they see which has the least? About how much more is the highest category? Can the students easily see if it's double, triple, or quadruple the number of the other categories?

Bar Graphs *(cont.)*

Lesson Directions

1. Explain that most times, people don't use sticky notes to create bar graphs. To make a bar graph, you must first collect data. Work with your class to collect data about another characteristic such as how many letters there are in students' names. On the board, write *four letters, five letters, six letters, seven letters,* and more than *seven letters*. Next to each category, tally the number of students whose names have that number of letters. When you are finished, explain that you have now collected data.

2. Display the Graph overhead and write the categories along the horizontal axis of the graph (*four letters, five letters, six letters, seven letters,* and *more than seven letters*) and numbers along the vertical axis. Work with the class to draw bars to represent your data. (Note: Remember to show the students how to read the graph—the bar goes up from the category but you read the number from the left.)

3. Again, evaluate the graph—is it easier to get information from the graph than it is from the data?

4. Explain that the students will be working in groups to collect data and show this data on bar graphs.

5. Divide the students into small groups. Distribute and review with the students "Bar Graphs" (page 56).

6. Work as a class to brainstorm possible things to graph. Examples include which of four movies students like most, what is their favorite food, what pets they have at home, how many siblings they have, etc. List these characteristics on the board.

7. Have each group pick something to graph.

8. Show the students how to use "Bar Graphs" (page 56) to collect data. Be sure to help the students list their categories on the sheet. Have the students gather data and list it on "Bar Graphs" (page 56)—this might include asking their classmates questions. This step can get a bit chaotic, so make sure to review your behavior expectations.

9. Have groups finish "Bar Graphs" (page 56) by graphing their results. Review again the procedure for turning data into graphs. This step is difficult, and you may need to offer guidance.

Lesson Closing

1. Using the graph on the board, the Graph overhead, or students' "Bar Graphs" (page 56), have the groups share their results with the class.

2. Ask each group to show their graph and explain three things they can determine by looking at the graph.

Written Assignment

Students will work in groups to create labeled Bar Graphs (page 56).

Bar Graphs *(cont.)*

Graph

Number

Categories

Bar Graphs *(cont.)*

Names _____ Date _____

Bar Graphs

Directions: Decide as a group what item you want to graph. Then collect your data and tally the results. Finally, make bar graphs to show your results.

1. What are you graphing? _____

2. Collecting Data

   What are your categories?

   Category 1: _____

   Category 2: _____

   Category 3: _____

   Category 4: _____

3. Put a mark for each student who fits the category.

4. Graphing

Bar Graphs *(cont.)*

Grading Rubric: Bar Graphs

Name _____   **Date** _____

Assignment	Points Possible	Points Earned
"Bar Graphs" (page 56)	Questions (10)	
	Graph (10)	
Oral Presentation	Preparation (10)	
	Delivery (10)	
Participation in Activity	Group Teamwork (10)	
	Participation in Lessons and Discussion (10)	
	Total Points Possible: 60	**Points Earned:**

Grading Rubric: Bar Graphs

Name _____   **Date** _____

Assignment	Points Possible	Points Earned
"Bar Graphs" (page 56)	Questions (10)	
	Graph (10)	
Oral Presentation	Preparation (10)	
	Delivery (10)	
Participation in Activity	Group Teamwork (10)	
	Participation in Lessons and Discussion (10)	
	Total Points Possible: 60	**Points Earned:**

Five Senses

Overview

Students will use their five senses to observe the natural world. They will then use the Writing Process and one of the four types of writing (expository, descriptive, persuasive, narrative) to record their observations.

Subjects	Writing, Science
Materials	• Colored Pens • Picture book with description of the natural world (see Lesson Opening, page 59) • "Five Senses Graphic Organizer" (page 61), "Four Types of Writing Slips" (page 62), and "Grading Rubric: Five Senses" (page 63)
Time	Two 50-minutes periods
Preparation	1. Copy and cut out enough "Four Types of Writing Slips" (page 62) so that each student has one. 2. Make one copy of "Five Senses Graphic Organizer" (page 61) and "Grading Rubric: Five Senses" (page 63) for each student.

Written Assignment: A short writing piece/illustration using one of the four types of writing and information from the five senses

Objectives

As a result of this activity, the students will:

- practice their skills of scientific observation
- explore four types of writing (expository, descriptive, narrative, persuasive)

Standards

Writing

1–All; 2–A; 3–All; 5–A, B, C, E, F

Science

As a result of activities in grades K–4, all students should develop:

- abilities necessary to do scientific inquiry
- an understanding of organisms and environments

Five Senses *(cont.)*

Lesson Opening

1. Read a picture book of your choice that includes a description of the natural world. The following books work well:

   • *Owl Moon* by Jane Yolen (Philomel, 1987)

   • *The Fall of Freddie the Leaf* by Leo Buscaglia (Slack, 2002)

   • *Night in the Country* by Cynthia Rylant (Alladin, 1991)

   • *Voices in the Park* by Anthony Browne (DK Children, 2001)

   • *Stranger in the Woods: A Photographic Fantasy* by Carl R. Sams (Carl R. Sams II Photography, 1999)

   • *Hello, Harvest Moon* by Ralph Fletcher (Clarion Books, 2003)

2. Discuss with your class what the writer of the book had to do before writing this book—he or she had to actually notice these details about the natural world. Help the class see that the writers also had to use his or her skills of scientific observation and the five senses to discover the details to put in the book. (Revisit the book to find evidence of the five senses. What did the writer hear, smell, taste, touch, and see?)

Lesson Directions

1. The students will be using their observation skills to explore the natural world and use these observations in their own writing, just like the author of the book you used in the Lesson Opening (see above).

2. Give each student "Five Senses Graphic Organizer" (page 61) and review this sheet with them. Explain that the best items to list on this sheet are things that are not obvious to everybody. For each of the five senses, they should list something that other people might not notice. Also explain how you want the students to observe taste—maybe you will ask each student to bring you the thing they want to taste before actually putting it in their mouth, or ask them each to taste something that you know is safe such as part of a piece of grass.

3. Have the class follow you outside and assign each student to observe a small part of the playground or field. The more spread out students are, the better. Encourage them to be absolutely quiet, so that everyone can use his or her sense of hearing to observe the natural world.

Five Senses *(cont.)*

Lesson Directions *(cont.)*

4. Once the students have completed "Five Senses Graphic Organizer" (page 61), have them return to the classroom.

5. Explain that now each student has details to use in his or her writing and it is time to figure out what to write.

6. Explain that there are four main types of writing with big names. Today the students will use one of these types of writing, but ask them not to worry if they can't remember all the names. Define the types of writing as follows:

   • *Expository:* tells true events

   • *Narrative:* tells a story

   • *Descriptive:* describes something without telling a story

   • *Persuasive:* convinces people of something

7. Explain that each student will be using the details of "Five Senses Graphic Organizer" (page 61) to do one of these kinds of writing.

8. Have each student choose one of the Four Types of Writing Slips (page 62)—this is the type of writing he or she will be doing. Show the students that the slips have hints about how they might write their piece. Each piece of writing should include the following:

   • illustration

   • title

   • information from their five senses (or revise the number of senses based on your class level)

9. Allow time for the students to draft, revise, and publish their work. This will likely take a few class periods, and you will need to offer guidance.

Lesson Closing

1. Have each student read aloud his or her writing and use specifics from the writing type to praise it. For example, if the student had used descriptive writing, you might say, "Wow, while I was listening to you read, I knew exactly what it was like to be there!" If a student used persuasive writing, you might say, "Wow, that really made me want to . . . !"

2. Either display students' projects around the room or bind them in a nature booklet that you can copy and send home to parents.

Written Assignment

The students will work individually to create short writing pieces, based on scientific observation, the Writing Process, and one of the four types of writing.

Five Senses *(cont.)*

Name_____   Date _____

Five Senses Graphic Organizer

Directions: For each of the five senses, list something that other people might not notice. Follow your teacher's directions for the taste section on this page.

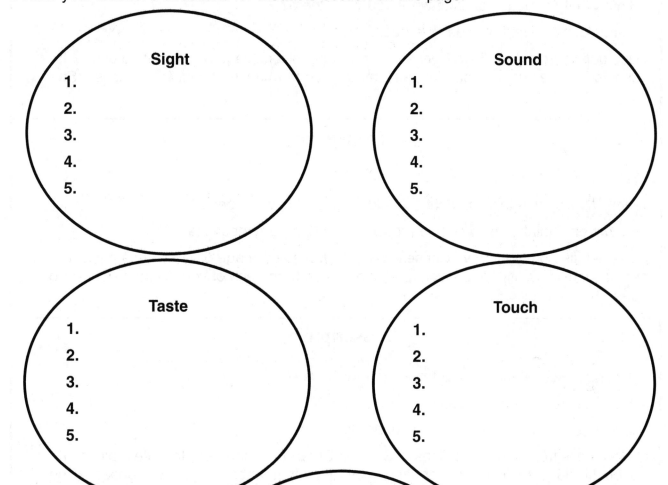

Sight
1.
2.
3.
4.
5.

Sound
1.
2.
3.
4.
5.

Taste
1.
2.
3.
4.
5.

Touch
1.
2.
3.
4.
5.

Smell
1.
2.
3.
4.
5.

Five Senses *(cont.)*

Four Types of Writing Slips

Expository

Tells true events

Hint: What happened outside while you were there?

Example: "We went outside. We heard . . . ."

Use details from your "Five Senses Graphic Organizer" (page 61) to write a piece. It should include a title, illustration, and information from each of your five senses. (See page 61.)

Persuasive

Tells people what to do

Hint: Why do you think students should respect school property?

Example: "I think people should respect school property because . . . ."

Use details from your "Five Senses Graphic Organizer" (page 61) to write a piece. It should include a title, illustration, and information from each of your five senses. (See page 61.)

Descriptive

Describes something without telling a story

Hint: This one is the easiest!

Example: "It looks like . . . ." "It sounds like . . . ."

Use details from your "Five Senses Graphic Organizer" (page 61) to write a piece. It should include a title, illustration, and information from each of your five senses. (See page 61.)

Narrative

Tells a story

Hint: Make up a story that happens outside.

Example: "One day I was building a snow fort outside and . . . ."

Use details from your "Five Senses Graphic Organizer" (page 61) to write a piece. It should include a title, illustration, and information from each of your five senses. (See page 61.)

Five Senses *(cont.)*

Grading Rubric: Five Senses

Name _____ Date _____

Assignment	Points Possible	Points Earned
"Five Senses Graphic" (page 56)	Completion (10)	
	Details (10)	
Four Types of Writing Assignment	Voice (5)	
	Organization (5)	
	Sentence Fluency (5)	
	Word Choice (5)	
	Ideas (5)	
	Conventions (5)	
	Presentation (5)	
Oral Presentation	Preparation (10)	
	Delivery (10)	
Participation in Activity	(25)	
Total Points Possible: 100		Points Earned:

Grading Rubric: Five Senses

Name _____ Date _____

Assignment	Points Possible	Points Earned
"Five Senses Graphic" (page 56)	Completion (10)	
	Details (10)	
Four Types of Writing Assignment	Voice (5)	
	Organization (5)	
	Sentence Fluency (5)	
	Word Choice (5)	
	Ideas (5)	
	Conventions (5)	
	Presentation (5)	
Oral Presentation	Preparation (10)	
	Delivery (10)	
Participation in Activity	(25)	
Total Points Possible: 100		Points Earned:

Sentence Relay

Overview

Working in teams, the students will race to write sentences using words chosen from a box. The first team to write six sentences wins. (Note: Instead of using the provided words, you may substitute content-area vocabulary from a recent unit of study.)

Subjects	Physical Education, Health
Materials	• One clipboard or other hard surface per team to use while standing • At least two pens or pencils per group • Container (e.g., box, hat) in which to place word slips • "Sentences" (page 66), "Word Slips" (pages 67–68), and "Grading Rubric: Sentence Relay" (page 69)
Time	One 50-minute period
Preparation	1. Mark a large circle (about 100-foot [30 m] diameter) in a field or gym and place the container at the center of this circle. 2. Make one copy per team of "Sentences" (page 66). 3. Make one copy of "Word Slips" (pages 67–68) and cut the slips out. If desired, laminate the page before copying. Place the slips in the container. 4. Make one copy of "Grading Rubric: Sentence Relay" (page 69) for each student.
Written Assignment: Word-Bank Sentences	

Objectives

As a result of this activity, the students will:

• cooperatively work as a team
• generate sentences based on a word bank
• be physically active

Standards

Writing

1–G; 3–All; 5–A, B, C, D

Physical Education

A physically educated student:

• demonstrates understanding and respect for differences among people in a physically active setting
• demonstrates responsible personal and social behavior in physically active settings

Sentence Relay *(cont.)*

Lesson Opening

1. Explain the following rules of the Sentence Relay:

   - Each team will line up outside the circle (teams spread out along the circle's circumference).

   - The relay consists of running to the middle of the circle to get a word slip and running back to the outside to write a sentence with your group before the next person in the group may go.

   - The sentences may be long or short, but they must include the word that the runner retrieved from the middle of the circle.

   - The team must work together to write the sentences, or the teacher may assign penalty seconds.

   - The first team to get through all the people in their group wins. (If there is an uneven number of team numbers, have smaller teams send one person twice.)

   - Explain that you will also give a point for the most creative sentence.

Lesson Directions

1. Divide the students into teams of five and have them line up outside the circle. Give each team a clipboard with a "Sentences" (page 66) sheet and pens or pencils attached. Allow time for groups to put their names on "Sentences" (page 66).

2. Point out the playing field and the word-bank box. Then review the game rules.

3. Have the teams play the Sentence Relay. Repeat with same or different teams as time allows. If desired, have the students choose two word slips at a time and use both words in the same sentence.

Lesson Closing

1. Once the game is over, give the winning team a classroom reward of your choice.

2. Ask the groups to share with the class sentences they especially liked.

Written Assignment

The students will work in groups to write sentences that include an assigned word.

Sentence Relay *(cont.)*

Names _____ Date _____

Sentences

1. _____
2. _____
3. _____
4. _____
5. _____
6. _____
7. _____
8. _____
9. _____
10. _____
11. _____
12. _____
13. _____
14. _____

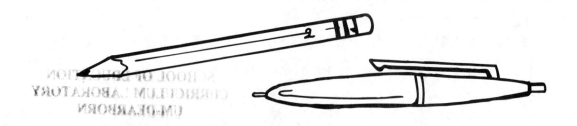

Sentence Relay *(cont.)*

Word Slips

Note to Teacher: If desired, replace these words with content-area vocabulary of your choice.

ladybug	**skateboard**
flying	**teacher**
brother	**bubble gum**
eraser	**soccer ball**
recess	**pizza**

Sentence Relay *(cont.)*

Word Slips

Note to Teacher: If desired, replace these words with content-area vocabulary of your choice.

new shoes	tractor
computer	tripped
snowing	banana
sailboat	backpack
rainy	Friday

Sentence Relay *(cont.)*

Grading Rubric: Sentence Relay

Name		Date

Assignment	Points Possible	Points Earned
"Sentences" (page 68)	Complete Sentences (10)	
	Conventions (10)	
	Used Word-Bank Word (10)	
	Creativity (10)	
Participation	Teamwork (10)	
	Effort (10)	
	Total Points Possible: 60	**Points Earned:**

Grading Rubric: Sentence Relay

Name		Date

Assignment	Points Possible	Points Earned
"Sentences" (page 68)	Complete Sentences (10)	
	Conventions (10)	
	Used Word-Bank Word (10)	
	Creativity (10)	
Participation	Teamwork (10)	
	Effort (10)	
	Total Points Possible: 60	**Points Earned:**

Butterfly Life Cycle

Overview

Students sequence pictures that represent the life cycle of the butterfly, write descriptions of each stage, and organize these stages on a decorated poster.

Subjects	Writing, Science
Materials	• Crayons, colored pencils, or colored pens • One sheet of poster paper for each student • Picture book that includes background information on the butterfly life cycle (see Lesson Opening, page 71) • Overhead projector and transparency • "Butterfly Poster" (page 72), "Butterfly!" (page 73), and "Grading Rubric: Butterfly Life Cycle" (page 74)
Time	Two 50-minute periods
Preparation	1. Make one copy of "Butterfly!" (page 73) and "Grading Rubric: Butterfly Life Cycle" (page 75) for each student. 2. Copy the "Butterfly Poster" (page 72) onto a transparency.

Written Assignment: Butterfly Life Cycle Poster

Objectives

As a result of this activity, the students will:

- learn the life cycle of the butterfly
- practice descriptive writing skills

Standards

Writing

1–A, C, E, G; 2–A; 3–All; 5–A, B, C, D, F, G

Science

As a result of activities in grades K–2, all students should develop an understanding of:

- the characteristics of organisms
- the life cycle of organisms
- organisms and environments

Butterfly Life Cycle *(cont.)*

Lesson Opening

Use one of the following picture books or your own resources to offer the students background information about the life cycle of the butterfly:

- *From Caterpillar to Butterfly* by Deborah Heiligman (HarperTrophy, 1996)

- *Becoming Butterflies* by Anne Rockwell (Walker Books for Young Readers, 2002)

- *Waiting for Wings* by Lois Ehlert (Harcourt Children's Books, 2001)

- *Charlie the Caterpillar* by Dom Deluise (Alladin Picture Books, 1993)

- *Where Butterflies Grow* by Joanne Ryder (Puffin, 1996)

Lesson Directions

1. Give each student "Butterfly!" (page 73) and have him or her cut out the four squares (or precut these before the activity).

2. Have each student color the four stages of the butterfly life cycle.

3. The students should work individually to sequence the four stages, laying them out on their desks.

4. Check that each student has correctly placed the four stages in order; then discuss the four stages as a class. Use the following vocabulary to describe a butterfly's life cycle:

    The butterfly develops through a process called *metamorphosis*, which means "change in shape." There are other insects that also go through metamorphosis. There are four stages in the development of a butterfly:

---

1. An adult female butterfly lays many eggs on a plant.

2. An egg hatches into a caterpillar or larva.

3. When the caterpillar has fully grown, it attaches to a place. The caterpillar forms a chrysalis.

4. The chrysalis develops into an adult butterfly.

---

5. Display the Butterfly Poster overhead and have the students use this as a model to create their own posters.

6. Discuss the term descriptive writing and ask each student to write a description of each stage of the butterfly's life under the corresponding picture. With less experienced classes, you might have the students draft these descriptions on scratch paper before transferring them to their posters. Give the students sheets of poster paper and allow them time to complete the project.

Butterfly Life Cycle *(cont.)*

Lesson Closing

1. Display the students' posters in the classroom.

2. Ask the students if they have ever seen these stages in real life. If possible, show the students examples of a chrysalis. (Optional: Use this activity to start a butterfly unit that includes keeping a chrysalis in the classroom and waiting for it to hatch.)

3. Discuss the differences between the butterfly's life cycle and our own life cycle.

Written Assignment

Each student will create a Butterfly Life Cycle Poster.

Butterfly Poster

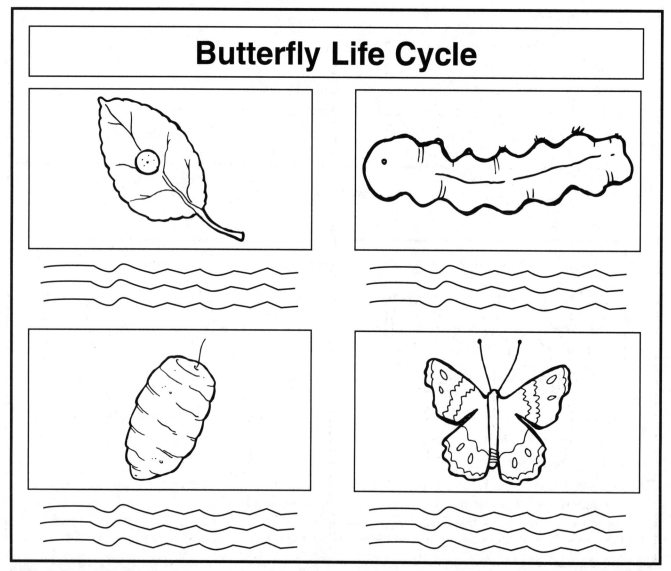

Butterfly Life Cycle *(cont.)*

Butterfly!

Butterfly Life Cycle *(cont.)*

Grading Rubric: Butterfly Life Cycle

Name _____ Date _____

Assignment	Points Possible	Points Earned
Butterfly Life Cycle Poster	Voice (5)	
	Organization (5)	
	Sentence Fluency (5)	
	Word Choice (5)	
	Ideas (5)	
	Conventions (5)	
	Presentation (5)	
Participation in Activity	(25)	
	Total Points Possible: 60	Points Earned:

Grading Rubric: Butterfly Life Cycle

Name _____ Date _____

Assignment	Points Possible	Points Earned
Butterfly Life Cycle Poster	Voice (5)	
	Organization (5)	
	Sentence Fluency (5)	
	Word Choice (5)	
	Ideas (5)	
	Conventions (5)	
	Presentation (5)	
Participation in Activity	(25)	
	Total Points Possible: 60	Points Earned:

Dust Bowl Photography

Overview

Students will explore Dust Bowl photography of the Great Depression and use illustration or photography to represent their school and community.

Subjects	Writing, Social Studies, Art
Materials	• Illustrating supplies, disposable cameras, or digital cameras • Colored pens or pencils • Clipboard or another hard writing surface for each student to use while standing • Large sheet of paper (on which to mount illustration) for each student • Overhead projector and three transparencies • "Dust Bowl Photographs" (pages 78–80)
Time	At least three 50-minute periods
Preparation	1. If you need permission slips in order to take your students on a walking tour in the area around your school, start the process a week in advance of this activity. 2. Copy the "Dust Bowl Photographs" (pages 78–80) onto transparencies. 3. Make one copy of "Grading Rubric: Dust Bowl Photography" (page 81) for each student.
Written Assignment: Illustration and short story, using art images as prompts	

Objectives

As a result of this activity, the students will:

- learn about the time period of the Great Depression
- interact with primary source documents
- explore how illustrations and photographs can represent society

Standards

Writing

1–A, C, F, G; 3–All

Social Studies

K–2: Understands changes in community life over time.

Art

K–4: Knows how history, culture, and the visual arts can influence each other.

Dust Bowl Photography *(cont.)*

Lesson Opening

1. Ask the students, "What does a farm look like? What grows on a farm? What colors would you see on a farm? What do fields of corn or grain look like?"

2. Display Dust Bowl Photograph overhead (A) and ask the students how this photograph is different than their idea of a farm. What do they notice that is missing?

3. Explain that this photograph is by an artist named Dorothea Lange, who took pictures of a period of U.S. history called the Great Depression. During the Great Depression, farms like this were known as part of the "Dust Bowl." Ask the students why the names *Great Depression* and *Dust Bowl* are appropriate. Explain that during the Great Depression, lack of rain and strong winds blew away all the good dirt and farmers couldn't grow anything.

4. Display Dust Bowl Overhead (B) and ask the students, "What do you notice? What do you think life was like during the Great Depression? How can you tell? How do these photographs show what life was like during the Great Depression?"

5. Display Dust Bowl Overhead (C) and explain that this is a picture called "Migrant Mother," also taken by Dorothea Lange. Ask the students what Dorothea Lange has captured in this picture that tells us about the time period. Encourage the students to look for details!

Lesson Directions

1. The students will now create their own artwork that depicts today's time period. Depending on your students' skill level, use one of the following techniques:

   - Give each student a sheet of paper, colored pens, and a clipboard. Take your class on a walking tour of the area around your school and have each student draw a "photograph" of something that they think is representative of the way we live today (e.g., fast-food restaurant, kids on a swing set, field with flowers). Let the students know there is no right or wrong thing to draw; encourage the students to be creative. If you use this option, have the students look for and include the smallest details they can notice.

   - Use digital cameras (from students) to take pictures. (The students may need to share the cameras.) On your walking tour, have each student shoot five photographs and then download them to your classroom computer. When shooting photos in both this option and the next, make sure the students (or you) jot down the subject of each photograph to later match the students to their photos.

   - Purchase one or two disposable cameras and, on your walking tour, let each student shoot one photograph. Have these photos developed and give each student the photo he or she took.

2. As closely as possible, match each student with the photo (or illustration) he or she created.

3. If using photos, have the students mount their photo on a sheet of paper. Have them add a title and two or three descriptive sentences under the photo. Encourage the students to include details in their descriptions. Have the students decorate their projects.

Dust Bowl Photography *(cont.)*

Lesson Closing

1. Have the students present their photos or illustrations. Which details do the students think represent life now? What do they think would be different if the photo were taken 10 years ago? What might be different if the photo were taken 10 years in the future?

2. Compliment the students on the included details and have them compare their photos to the Dust Bowl Photographs shown on the overheads. What are the emotions captured in each scene? How do the students think the world is different now in comparison to during the Great Depression?

Written Assignment

Each student will create either an illustration or a photograph that represents the world of today, mount his or her artwork, add a title, and write a few descriptive sentences.

Dust Bowl Photography *(cont.)*

Dust Bowl Photographs (A)

Image courtesy of the Library of Congress

Dust Bowl Photography *(cont.)*

Dust Bowl Photographs (B)

Images courtesy of the Library of Congress

Dust Bowl Photography *(cont.)*

Dust Bowl Photographs (C)

Image courtesy of the Library of Congress

Dust Bowl Photography *(cont.)*

Grading Rubric: Dust Bowl Photography		
Name		**Date**
Assignment	**Points Possible**	**Points Earned**
Dust Bowl Artwork (either illustration or photograph)	Presentation (10)	
	Effort (10)	
Dust Bowl Writing	Voice (5)	
	Organization (5)	
	Sentence Fluency (5)	
	Word Choice (5)	
	Ideas (5)	
	Conventions (5)	
	Presentation (5)	
Participation in Activity	(25)	
	Total Points Possible: 80	**Points Earned:**

Grading Rubric: Dust Bowl Photography		
Name		**Date**
Assignment	**Points Possible**	**Points Earned**
Dust Bowl Artwork (either illustration or photograph)	Presentation (10)	
	Effort (10)	
Dust Bowl Writing	Voice (5)	
	Organization (5)	
	Sentence Fluency (5)	
	Word Choice (5)	
	Ideas (5)	
	Conventions (5)	
	Presentation (5)	
Participation in Activity	(25)	
	Total Points Possible: 80	**Points Earned:**

Puzzling Shapes

Overview

Students will work in groups, manipulating geometric shapes to create given puzzle images. Students will then create their own puzzles and trade with friends to try to solve the puzzles. Whenever a student solves a puzzle, he or she will brainstorm and write the guess of what the puzzle is supposed to be. The lesson closes with group brainstorming and a discussion of Brainstorming as the first step of the Writing Process.

Subjects	Writing, Art, Math
Materials	• Scissors and colored pens or pencils • One sheet of white paper for each student • "Tangram Template" (page 84), "Tangram Cat" (page 85), "Tangram Puzzles" (page 86), "Tangram Answers" (page 87), and "Grading Rubric: Puzzling Shapes" (page 88) • Overhead projector and two transparencies
Time	Two 50-minute periods
Preparation	1. Copy "Tangram Cat" (page 85) and "Tangram Answers" (page 87) onto transparencies. 2. Make one copy per group of "Tangram Template" (page 84) and "Tangram Puzzles" (page 86). 3. Make one copy of "Tangram Template" (page 84) and "Grading Rubric: Puzzling Shapes" (page 88) for each student.
Written Assignment: Tangram Puzzle and Written Brainstorms	

Objectives

As a result of this activity, the students will:

- experiment with geometric shapes
- practice brainstorming as the first step of the Writing Process

Standards

Writing

1–A, D, E, G; 5–A, C, D

Art

K–4: Uses visual structures and functions of art to communicate ideas.

Math

K–2: Understands that patterns can be made by putting different shapes together or taking them apart.

Puzzling Shapes *(cont.)*

Lesson Opening

1. Divide students into groups of three and give each group a "Tangram Template" (page 84). Allow them time to color and cut out the pieces.

2. Display the Tangram Cat overhead and work with groups to arrange their pieces into the shape of the cat shown.

3. Give each group "Tangram Puzzles" (page 86) and give them time to create the pictures using the pieces. Which group will be first to create each shape?

Lesson Directions

1. Give each student "Tangram Template" (page 84) and give him or her time to color and cut out the pieces.

2. Explain that the students will be using their tangram shapes to create a picture of their choice. Then they will trace that outline onto a sheet of white paper.

3. Allow time for students to manipulate their shapes and trace their finished puzzle (you might need to help with this!).

4. Have the students keep their tangram pieces but trade puzzle outlines. Ask them *not* to tell their friends what their tangram shape is supposed to be!

5. When a person solves a tangram puzzle, have him or her write on the page what the student thinks it is (e.g., boat, horse, pumpkin). Continue passing around the tangram puzzles and allowing time for the students to solve them—again, whenever a student solves a puzzle, he or she should write his or her guess on the puzzle. Ask them not to list something that has already been guessed— they may need to brainstorm and be creative to come up with unused ideas, especially as you get further into the activity.

Lesson Closing

1. At the end of the activity, each student's tangram puzzle should include at least a few ideas as to what the puzzle actually is supposed to be.

2. Have the students present their puzzles to the class, explaining what they meant the puzzles to be. Then, have the class brainstorm other possibilities. Explain that *Brainstorming* is the first part of the Writing Process. Now that students have brainstormed, they should be able to write stories about their puzzles.

Written Assignment

Each student will create a tangram puzzle and brainstorm in writing what his or her friends' puzzles are supposed to be.

Puzzling Shapes *(cont.)*

Tangram Template

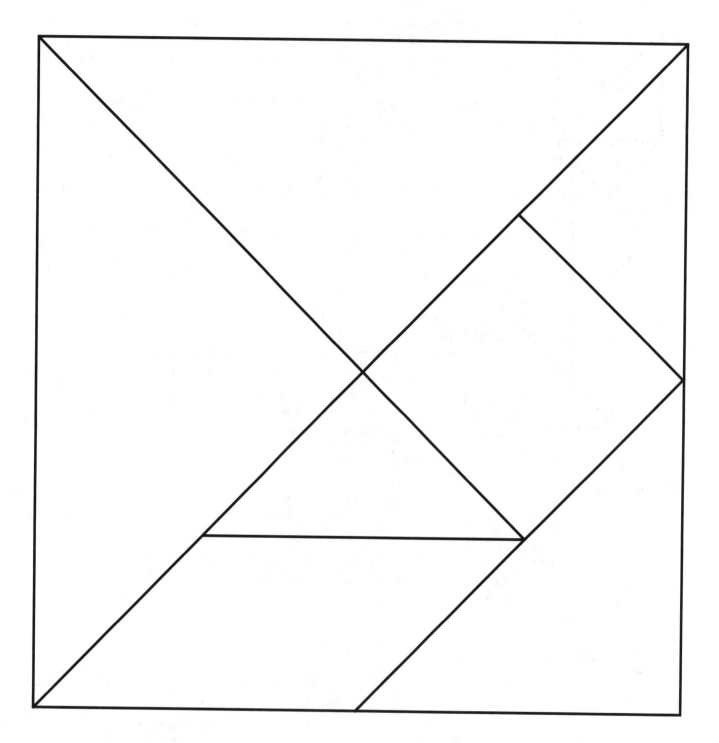

Puzzling Shapes *(cont.)*

Tangram Cat

Puzzling Shapes (cont.)

Tangram Puzzles

Names _____ Date _____

Directions: Use your tangram pieces from page 84. Work as a group to create each shape on this page. When you have created a shape, fill in the circle next to it.

Puzzling Shapes *(cont.)*

Tangram Answers

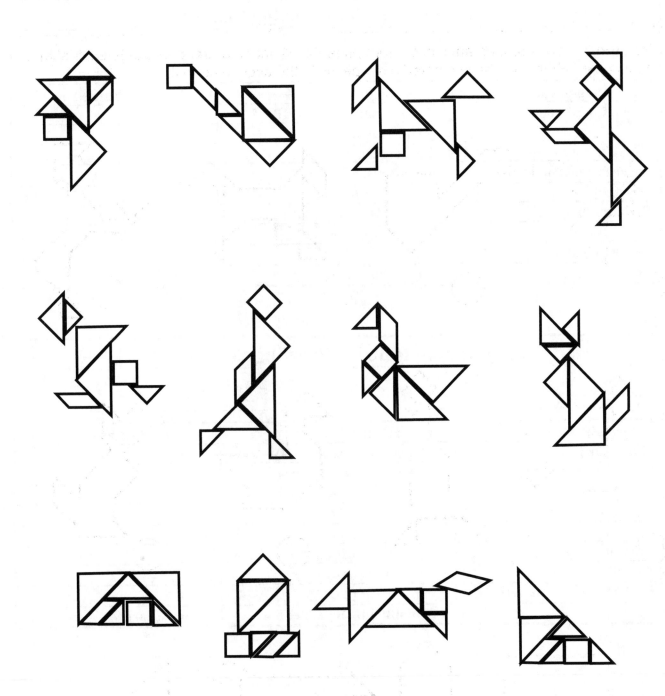

Puzzling Shapes *(cont.)*

Grading Rubric: Puzzling Shapes

Name _____ **Date** _____

Assignment	Points Possible	Points Earned
Group Cooperation	In creating shapes (10)	
	In manipulating shapes to Creating tangram puzzles (10)	
Finished Tangram Puzzle	Presentation (10)	
	Effort (10)	
Brainstorming	In Discussion (10)	
	In Writing (10)	
Participation in Activity	(25)	
	Total Points Possible: 85	**Points Earned:**

Grading Rubric: Puzzling Shapes

Name _____ **Date** _____

Assignment	Points Possible	Points Earned
Group Cooperation	In creating shapes (10)	
	In manipulating shapes to Creating tangram puzzles (10)	
Finished Tangram Puzzle	Presentation (10)	
	Effort (10)	
Brainstorming	In Discussion (10)	
	In Writing (10)	
Participation in Activity	(25)	
	Total Points Possible: 85	**Points Earned:**

Graphic Organizers for Any Occasion

This Week (page 90)

Use this chart to help the students plan each day of their week.

Big Idea/Little Ideas (page 91)

Have the students write a main idea in the top bubble and then list things that relate to this idea in the three bubbles below. This is a great way to narrow down a topic or prewrite a short piece.

Concept Wheel (page 92)

Have the students write a main idea in the center and brainstorm related thoughts in the outside sections of the wheel. This is a more advanced version of the Big Idea/Little Ideas graphic organizer.

Venn Diagram (page 93)

Use this graphic organizer to help the students compare and contrast two things or ideas. The students should write the commonalities in the space shared by both circles, and the traits unique to each item in that item's circle.

Storyboard (page 94)

This chart is useful when asking the students to plan a piece of writing that includes a storyline. Have the students use the boxes to illustrate a sequence of events before trying to write these events in words.

KWL Chart (page 95)

Use this organizer before and then after a lesson. Before the lesson, ask the students to write what they Know about the topic and what they Wonder about the topic. After the lesson, ask the students what they have Learned.

Cause and Effect (page 96)

Use this chart to help the students link cause and effect. This is especially useful when evaluating literature, making health decisions, or exploring causality during a science lesson.

This Week

Monday	
Tuesday	
Wednesday	
Thursday	
Friday	
Over the Weekend	

Big Idea/Little Ideas

Big Idea

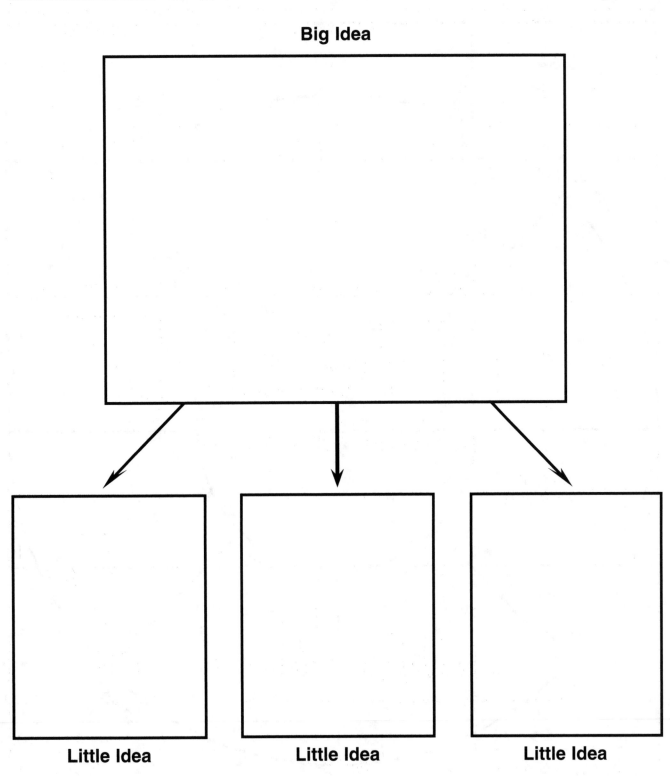

Little Idea   **Little Idea**   **Little Idea**

Concept Wheel

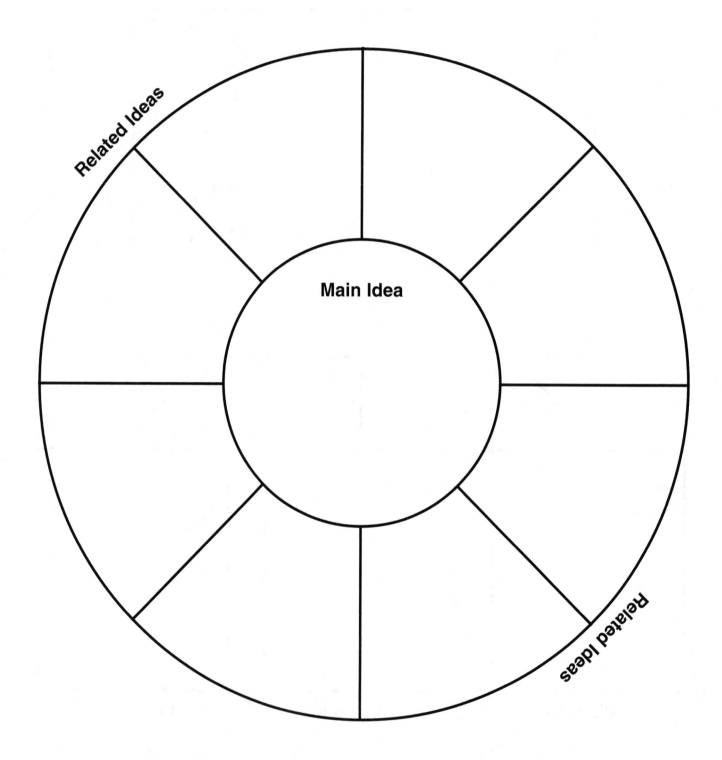

Related Ideas

Main Idea

Related Ideas

Venn Diagram

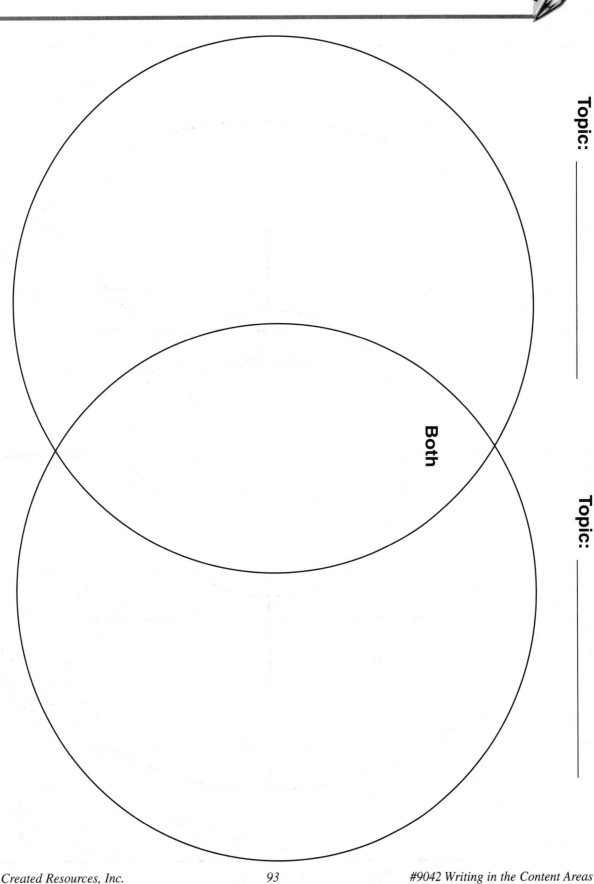

Topic: _____

Topic: _____

Both

Storyboard

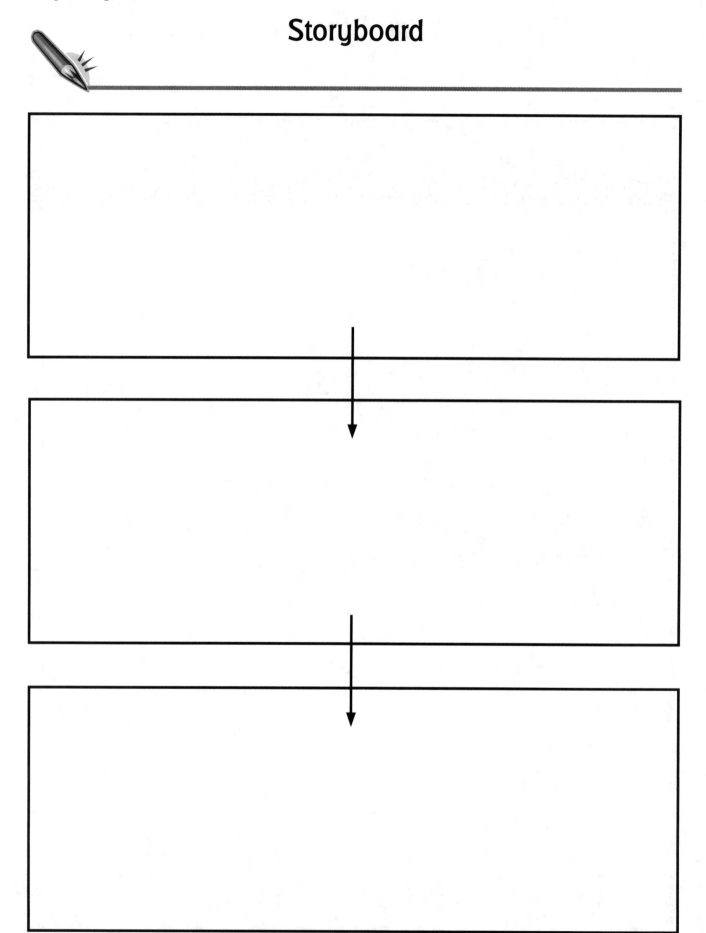

KWL Chart

Topic: _____

Know	Wonder	Learned

Cause and Effect

Topic:_____

Cause

Cause

↓

↓

Effect

Effect

Cause

Cause

↓

↓

Effect

Effect